W9-AKY-263

To

_____

From

_____

JIMMY WAYNE

Ruby
THE
FOSTER
DOG

Illustrations by Muza Ulasowski

BroadStreet
KIDS

Published by BroadStreet Kids
BroadStreet Kids is an imprint of

BroadStreet Publishing® Group, LLC
Racine, Wisconsin USA
BroadStreetPublishing.com

Ruby the Foster Dog

ISBN-13: 978-1-4245-5408-9 (hardcover)
ISBN-13: 978-1-4245-5439-3 (e-book)

Stock or custom editions of BroadStreet Publishing titles may be purchased in bulk for educational, business, ministry, fundraising, or sales promotional use. For information, please e-mail info@ broadstreetpublishing.com.

Editorial services provided by Ginger Garrett and Jackie Marushka
Cover and interior by Garborg Design Works at garborgdesign.com
Illustrations by Muza Ulasowski at muzadesigns.com

Printed in China
17 18 19 20 21 5 4 3 2 1

For
Ruby

CHAPTER ONE

The tornado siren screamed.

The small farming community just outside of White Deer, Texas, was under attack. Violent, whirling winds roared as rain slammed against the window in the dark office across the hallway. A bazillion bright bolts of lightning lit up the greenish-yellow sky.

I could see flashes of the fat funnel spinning in my direction. The employees at the animal shelter had already escaped. They had run for cover in a nearby underground cellar.

I couldn't escape. I was locked in a small cage, just like all the other dogs trapped inside the shelter. All I could do was curl up under my towel and close my eyes.

There were more lightning strikes, followed by deafening booms that shook the walls. The tornado roared toward us like a speeding freight train, the eerie sound of a phantom engine screaming past.

The floor and walls all around me squeaked and cracked. I peeked out from underneath my towel, almost expecting to see a ghost train bearing down on us. I saw only darkness and lightning strikes clawing at the earth.

There was a loud crash, and wind rushed through the broken window in the office across the hall, filling the shelter with warm air, causing the roof to lift off like a balloon. I could see the beams straining to hold on, to resist the overwhelming force fighting against them. What gave them their strength? How could they hold on?

The howls and cries from the other dogs scared me. The dog in the cage next to me frantically clawed at the door, desperate to escape.

The window blinds flapped then ripped free from the window. They slammed against the wall and fell. The wind yanked my towel away, trying to yank it through the bars of my cage.

The wind continued bullying the roof, pushing and pulling it like bullies do, but the nails would not give in. They held on to the rafters with all their might.

Finally the wind gave up. The roof relaxed. The walls stopped bending and the floors stopped moving under me. The tornado was gone. Bright sunlight split the dark sky.

I stood up and shook the glass and debris off my body, then looked around.

Carefully walking to the cage door, I stuck my nose through the wire as far as it would go. The air smelled like diesel fuel and sawdust. I looked up and down the hall. Was anyone out there? All the other dogs were sticking their noses through their doors and looking up and down the hall too. Every dog in the shelter was terrified and confused— even the older, bigger dogs. We needed our people.

Hours went by. Finally, I heard someone opening the front door of the shelter.

It was one of the employees. We were safe! We all barked and yelped, wagging our tails. One by one, the employees entered the shelter. They slowly walked past our cages, glancing inside to see if we were alive.

We were, but we were quivering and in shock. We needed to be held.

The phone rang. An employee answered. Someone's family was calling to make sure everyone was okay. All afternoon, the employees called their families, and their families called them. Each employee shared a story and even reenacted their near-death escape from the tornado. Each described how they had made it to the underground shelter just in time.

All the dogs stood at their cage doors, eavesdropping.

"We're lucky to be alive," one employee said. "I can't wait to go home and hug my family."

I barked, but they weren't listening. The dogs were lucky to be alive too! Why hadn't they taken us to the underground shelter? Didn't they care about us? No one even seemed to notice we needed comfort. No one remembered we didn't have families. We felt invisible, and in some ways, that scared us more than the tornado.

The employees gathered in the office across the hall, complaining about the broken window. Glass was everywhere. The tornado had left them with a big mess.

I looked down at my paw. A little piece of glass had blown into the cage and cut my toe. I hadn't felt any pain when it happened, but now I did.

No one noticed that, either.

An employee grabbed a broom and started cleaning.

"At least no one got hurt," he said, then whistled as he worked.

Within a few hours, things seemed back to normal around the shelter.

But life inside a shelter is anything but normal.

A musky, vinegary smell constantly lingered throughout the room. It was always cold as a cave but not nearly as quiet. Dogs begged for attention night and day. The thin, light-blue towel I was given to lie on barely kept me warm. I shivered whenever I tried to sleep.

I wanted out of here. I wanted a family.

The second hand on a big clock near the fire exit ticked, sounding like a sledgehammer slamming down on a steel railroad spike. Each tick echoed down the gray hallways where the cages were stacked. One on top of the other, we were stuck inside the cages like containers on cargo ships, as if people wanted to get rid of us one way or the other.

Inside each cage was a sad, innocent dog. Not one of us had done anything wrong. None of us deserved this.

This place was called a shelter, but we didn't feel protected. My cage had a big lock on the outside of the door. The cage's ceiling, walls, and floor were made of dark metal bars that made a fence all the way around. I was a prisoner, not a pet.

The cage wasn't just ugly. It hurt. My little toes got trapped in the fenced floor when I tried to walk. My paws hurt if I stood too long too. I tried to stand anyway, though, staring through the bars at visitors whenever they walked by.

I overheard one of the employees at the shelter saying he'd visited Alcatraz Island. He said it had a prison on it, and the prisoners were allowed to leave their cells, go outside, and get a breath of fresh air from time to time.

I envied them. The only sunlight I ever saw was through the office window when the blinds weren't closed and pulled down. On a good day, the blinds were open and the sun was out. Then I could see the green trees covered with leaves. In the distance, I could see green grass and people smiling as they walked by with their dogs on leashes.

I wish I had someone who loved me. If I had a family who

loved me, I would be the best dog in the world. We would go on long walks and live in a big house.

I continued standing on the fenced floor, staring through the window, daydreaming. Sometimes I dreamed of escaping to freedom. Most days, though, I just dreamed about having a family.

The hardest part about making up a good daydream? You have to know exactly what you're dreaming of.

I didn't know what families were like. I didn't know what it felt like to be loved. Sometimes I wondered if my daydreams would ever come true. Part of me knew that wishes weren't nails. Wishes never held anything together.

I wondered how many things I didn't know. And there was one mystery that troubled me more than all the rest combined.

Every day, dogs disappeared from this place.

The luckiest dogs left the shelter to join a family.

Every day, someone new visited the shelter looking for a dog to adopt. People usually came in with ideas about who the perfect dog would be. Two sweet grandparents wanted a furry, friendly sheepdog for their grandkids. One nice man wanted a sweet lab pup to surprise his wife for an anniversary. An elderly gentleman wanted a calm, older dog to keep him company while he worked in the yard.

Visitors like that always walked slowly up and down the hallway. They stopped in front of each stack of cages, looking at the dog in the cage on the top and then looking at the dog in the cage in the middle and then in the bottom cage. They acted like they were in the produce department at the grocery store. I'm surprised no one squeezed us to see if we were ripe.

The worst part of the experience? Listening to what they said. They always made comments about our appearance.

"How cute!"

"How pretty!"

"That's one ugly dog."

"We want a boy, not a girl."

They commented on each one of us, then moved on to the next stack of cages and did the same thing all over again. They wanted a dog just like the one in their imaginations. No matter how high I jumped or how hard I wagged my tail, no one wanted a dog like me.

Sometimes people came to look at us, but they didn't even plan to adopt anyone. They'd just look at us, sigh, then mosey on out of the shelter and go on with their lives. We always wondered why they came to look at dogs they didn't want to help.

Waiting to be adopted was hard. It was like waiting to see a shooting star or waiting for Christmas morning. I'd heard about Christmas from the shelter employees. I wanted to open presents someday too.

Every day, every minute, and every second dragged on like a three-toed sloth.

Actually, I think a three-toed sloth would move faster.

Rocks would be more affectionate than the shelter's employees were. I wish I could call them by their names, but they wore their badges high up on their shirts. I was never a very good reader anyway.

They didn't want to be friends with us, though. They were like big, weathered trees on top of a high, lonely mountain. They kept themselves out of reach in every way.

When a new employee started to pet me, another guy,

an employee with a bald head and long neck, stopped him. "Don't get attached!" he warned. Then he nodded to the big, black door at the end of the hallway.

Dogs disappeared through that door. The employees knew all about it, I realized.

"What's behind that door?" the new guy asked.

"We call it the 'room of no return.' Sometimes the cutest dogs are sent to a bigger shelter where they have a better chance of being adopted. But other dogs … " His voice lowered and he looked around.

I strained to hear what he said, but I couldn't. The new guy shuddered and walked away.

The bald guy with the long neck grabbed a card off a cage and sighed. "Two more days for you, fella. Too bad you're so ugly. Your eighteen days are almost up."

I growled. That guy was no beauty himself.

That's when I noticed the cards above the cages. Each card had two numbers: the dog's identification number and a date. The date was the day that the dog went into the cage.

Until now, I hadn't realized why that date was so important.

A dog only had eighteen days to make it out of here. After that, he disappeared behind the black door.

I pushed my nose against the metal bars of my cage, desperate to see the number written on my card. How many days did I have left?

That night I tried to sleep, but I kept crying for all the innocent dogs that would never see day nineteen.

What would make any human being treat an innocent dog like that? A dog always loves unconditionally. Doesn't everyone want to be loved? Don't they know what they're missing?

I rolled over, trying to get comfortable on my towel. The room was cold, and I could hear dogs whimpering in their sleep. They were having bad dreams, too, I guess.

I fell back asleep, dreaming about dogs taking over the world and licking every kid's face off. That was a good dream. Except that I liked kids. And I didn't know if I wanted to lick anyone's face off. I'd heard that kids were dirty. I don't mind licking my paws, but at least I know where they've been.

In the darkness, I waited for the sun to rise, and thought about life. When God created this world, He didn't make roads, shopping centers, and dog shelters. He made beautiful places to live and a blue sky to run under.

Humans built all those ugly concrete things, sticking them everywhere. So why should dogs be locked in cages or chained and not allowed to roam free? It's our world too. And we do a pretty good job with it. When is the last time a dog started a war between two countries over religion? When is the last time a dog judged someone for the color of his skin? Plus, dogs don't just love; they are smart and brave too.

Dogs are great. It's people that need a little work.

CHAPTER TWO

The shelter employees gave me three things: a light-blue towel to lie on and cover up with, a collar, and a tag inscribed with the number 127. The tag was scratched and bent, and the collar was so long the end of it flopped over and nearly touched the floor. A bigger dog than me once wore it, that's for sure. I wondered how that dog's story ended.

After the employees had gone home for the night, I asked around about the dog whose days were up. No one admitted knowing who he was or what happened to him. But once I started asking questions, everyone started to talk.

During the day, we had to focus on trying to be adopted, so we didn't converse much. And with the metal dividers between each cage, we had to stretch our necks to get a good look at each other. But tonight, everyone felt like a friend. We were companions, not competitors.

First, Parker the Barker introduced himself. He was a black-and-white dog in the cage to my left. In his youth, he'd had black hair. Old age had given him plenty of white hair. His number was 117,

but I called him Parker the Barker because he barked all the time. He barked at his tail. He barked at the volunteers. He even barked in his sleep.

"You're probably wondering how a dog as handsome as me could be brought so low," he said, looking around his cage.

I was actually wondering if he ever stopped barking, but I just nodded.

"My owner was an elderly woman who passed away. Her children sold her house and dropped me off at the shelter. Can you imagine? Dropped off, just like a donation to Goodwill!" He growled, reliving the memory. "I've been here ever since, waiting for someone to adopt me. The problem is, I only appeal to people with excellent taste. They tend to be few and far between."

The dog to my right started laughing. She wouldn't stop, and then I started laughing even though I tried to stop. Parker the Barker barked at us, and we girls laughed even harder. Finally, he started laughing too.

"I'm Stella," the dog to my right said. "Around here they call me 823. I hope that's a good number."

"I'm sure it is," I said, trying to be helpful. I already liked her, even though we had never talked before.

"I didn't have an owner, not like Parker. I did have puppies, though, lots and lots of them. New litters every year … until … " Her voice wavered.

"Until what?" I asked. My stomach felt funny, as if her story mattered more than I knew.

"I got old." She sighed a big, loud, long sigh. "I tried not to, but it happened anyway. Then the breeder didn't want me anymore."

I craned my neck around and got a good look at her. She was a Chihuahua, just like me! Her ears were pointy, her legs were short, and her tail curled up. She would have been just perfect, except she didn't have an underbite like mine.

She was so sweet and very humble too. All the dogs talked for hours and told wild stories. Stella didn't talk a lot, but when she did, it was always about how much she missed her pups. They were all taken from her and sold to strangers by the puppy-mill owner. Even though it hurt my paws, I stood up in my cage and pressed my nose against the bars. She did the same.

As dawn drew close, Stella and I curled up in our cages. Parker the Barker still wanted to talk, though.

"Let me tell you about the good old days. In the summer, I used to roll in the mud and jump into a kiddy pool every day. At Christmas, I'd rip open my presents with my teeth, and when the snow came, you'd find me lying by the fireplace. I looked just like this." He struck a royal-looking pose, his head held high, his black nose twitching.

Stella stifled a giggle. She must have had a better view of him than I did.

"And I traveled too. First class, always. I've walked the streets of New York City and visited Central Park. There was a thing called a carousel that went around and around, and children rode on the backs of horses, tigers, giraffes, and all kinds of other animals that had been frozen in time." He lowered his voice and whispered to Stella and me, "Can you imagine? Who would freeze an animal in time and let kids ride it in a park?"

I had no idea what he was talking about.

"Oh, and did I tell you about the pretzels?"

I didn't know what a pretzel was, but if I asked questions, he'd talk longer.

"They're delicious! The vendor parked his cart on the sidewalk in front of the Hearst building. You know the Hearst building, of course. It's the height of elegance. And I must really suggest you try the pretzels."

"Parker," I asked, "haven't you ever done normal stuff, like chase mailmen or growl at cats?" I clapped my paw over my mouth, but it was too late.

"Well, since you asked, one day, I was running down the beach, just minding my own business. I saw steps leading up to a big swimming pool, so I decided to take a dip. I carefully walked up the steps and looked to see if anyone was sitting around the pool. It was all clear, so I jumped into the pool and paddled from one side to the other, without a care in the world.

"All of a sudden, I heard a man yell, 'Get out of my pool!' He took the pool net and tried to grab me with it! I quickly swam to the opposite side. The man ran around to that side and tried to grab me again with the net. I then swam down to the shallow end and hurried out of the pool.

"The man met me there, and we stood facing each other. He moved toward me, and I turned and ran. He chased me around and around the pool, but it was hard for him to run with flip-flops on his feet. I stopped once again and looked back at the man. By now, he was sweating and breathing hard.

"It was obvious by the look on his face he was furious. He took off one of his flip-flops and threw it at me! Instead of immediately running away, though, I grabbed his flip-flop with my mouth and then took off running, back down the steps onto the beach. The man gave chase, but I was too fast. I ran figure eights and circles around the man, who was still yelling for me to drop his flip-flop. I finally let go of his flip-flop and ran back down the beach."

I didn't know what a flip-flop was, but Parker the Barker had sure made that man mad. Stella and I shook our heads.

"You were a bad boy, Parker the Barker," she said.

He laughed and laughed.

I guess I liked that story most of all because I wanted to be free and rebellious a little too. And who would have guessed that Parker had ever stolen a flip-flop?

"Most of the time," Parker said quietly, "being happy isn't about having adventures. The happiest days of my life were spent on the front porch, in the shade at my old house, watching the world go by. My owner—she was a grandmotherly, kindhearted lady—sat in her green chair, worked crossword puzzles, and sipped Coca-Cola. I loved her. I would trade all the pretzels and flip-flops in the world to be with her for just one more day."

I didn't have any stories to share because I was brought to the shelter when I was six weeks old. But I knew what I wanted. I wanted to ride down a long, red dirt road in a pickup truck with my nose sticking out the window and my ears flapping and my tongue lapping up the wind. I wanted to run on a soft Carolina beach and experience a little "flip-flop rhythm and summertime feeling," like Parker the Barker did. Most of all, I just wanted a safe home and someone I could love who would love me back.

Just before I fell asleep, I said a prayer. "God, please give me a family and a home." I prayed for Stella and Parker the Barker, too, and all the other dogs in the shelter, no matter what color, shape, or size they were. All dogs deserved love and a good home. Even dogs who stole a person's flip-flops.

🐾

A wonderful family, looking for an older dog they didn't have to house-train, finally adopted Parker the Barker. You should've heard him bark! He was so excited.

Two days later, a beautiful woman, who wanted a friend for her long-haired dachshund named Willie, adopted Stella. When he and Stella met, it was puppy love at first sight. She nibbled his ear and Willie rolled over on his back. I blushed. I didn't think I would ever want to nibble a dog's ear.

They wrestled the entire time it took the lady to sign the adoption papers. I wagged my tail, watching.

Stella and Parker lived to see Day 19. When they trotted out the door, I tried to wipe the tears off my snout, but they came too fast. I was happy, even though I was sad. Emotions don't always make a lot of sense.

I missed Stella and Parker the Barker so much, but I was glad they didn't have to live inside a cage any longer. I couldn't wait until someone would adopt me too. I would get hugs, belly rubs, suds in a tub, and all kinds of love. I still wasn't sure about the ear nibbles, though.

I spent several more days locked in the cage, watching other dogs come and go from the shelter. Sadness and loneliness became my two closest companions. I stopped standing on the fenced floor doing the routine I made up.

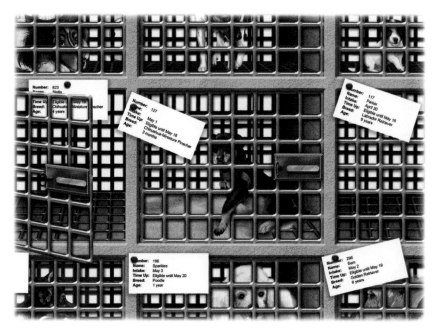

I called it the "bark bark stomp wiggle wagtail jig," and I did it every time a visitor came near my cage. Then, as my heart grew cold and hope died off, I just stared out of the bars and stopped moving at all.

I wasn't a bad dog. I just wasn't a wanted dog. Sometimes I looked down at the two heart-shaped brown spots on my chest, which I was born with, and sighed. No one ever looked close enough to see them. I had a lot of love to offer someone if they'd just give me a chance. But with each passing day, I was running out of chances … and time.

I would have never imagined that a man dressed like a snow skier, walking in the summer heat, would give me that chance.

◄ EXIT

Thar
for w

CHAPTER THREE

Stomp, stomp, stomp. I recognized the sound of heavy hiking boots clomping down the concrete hallway.

Click, clack, click, clack. My ears shot up. What was that sound? I strained to see around the metal cage divider.

Someone was walking toward my cage, using two poles as walking sticks. Who would use ski poles in the middle of summer?

The noises slowed down in front of my cage. I looked up, more interested in the poles than the man holding them. He was probably here for a big, athletic boy dog. Maybe a Husky, with its thick fur, made for snow.

The stranger looked at me and smiled. Then he walked away, just like every visitor had done before him.

No one wants me. Not even a goofy-looking man wearing ski goggles on top of his head.

I laid my head back down and closed my eyes. I wondered how many days I had left. Then I wondered why that man had come to a dog shelter. Was he lost? Was he crazy?

"That's the one I want, right there."

I opened my eyes. He was going to adopt someone. Who?

I slowly stood up, blinking, and saw the shaggy-haired, scruffy-faced man pointing directly at me.

Me?

A shelter employee unlocked the cage, reached in, picked me up, and handed me to the man. He had gloves on, and each glove had been cut off at the fingertips. His fingers were warm as he cradled me gently.

"Wanna go with me, girl?" he asked politely.

Go where? The North Pole?

"I'm not going home quite yet, though," he said.

I cocked my head to one side, confused.

"I'm walking halfway across America to raise awareness for foster children."

I wagged my tail, just once. I didn't know what a foster was, but I knew what children were, and I liked them very much.

"Why?" the employee asked.

The stranger turned to face the employee, still cradling me close. "Every year, kids age out of foster care. That means they don't have permanent families, but they're too old to live with a temporary family anymore. They end up homeless and hopeless."

The employee's face fell, as if he had a bad memory of being hopeless too. I wondered if everyone knew what that word felt like. Lots of people knew what it meant, but not everyone knows what it feels like.

The stranger looked down at me. "Anyway, if you're up for an adventure, I'd love the company."

I cocked my head to the other side. I wondered what Stella and Parker would have done. What was riskier: staying inside here another day or leaving with this crazy guy?

He patted his jacket. "You can ride right here in the top of my jacket if you want to."

I squirmed and wiggled, trying to escape. My idea of being adopted did not include a man walking halfway across America. My idea was a normal family with a nice comfortable house.

What kind of person would walk halfway across America anyway?

I glanced back at my cage, remembering how the bars hurt my paws, and how much I wanted to feel the sun again.

I guess riding shotgun in his jacket is better than being locked in a cage all the time.

I wagged my tail. But just once, and not hard. I didn't want to give him the wrong impression.

"Alrighty, then, let's go!" he said.

I hopped inside his gray jacket, and he zippered it up, leaving just enough room at the top for my head to stick out. The shaggy-haired man signed his name on the adoption form. I peeked at the form. His name was James. His hand hovered over a line that said "Dog Name."

He left it blank. Maybe he wasn't too sure about me, either.

The shelter employee handed him a small bag of dry dog food. The Salvation Army had delivered it to the shelter a week ago. Some wonderful people in the community had donated it to them. Mr. James seemed to be happy about that, because he took the bag and stuck it in a fanny pack he was wearing around his waist. He turned to leave.

"Don't forget her towel," the employee yelled out.

Mr. James put the towel in his backpack, said one last good-bye to the employees, and headed toward the front door of the shelter.

When Mr. James pushed open the front door, a beam of sunlight hit my eyes, nearly blinding me. My eyes were very sensitive from being indoors for so long. Quickly, I tucked my head inside Mr. James's jacket. I didn't know the sun could hurt my eyes.

What other surprises were in store?

Mr. James headed down the road, on foot. He had said he was walking halfway across America, but I had hoped I could ride in a car. Did we both have to walk? How long would that take? When would we reach home? Did he even have a home? I had so many worries, but I kept them to myself.

"Are you doing okay in there?" he asked, interrupting my panicked thoughts. Mr. James noticed I was hiding my face from the sunlight. I didn't say anything or move.

I continued hiding inside his jacket as he walked. Little by little, I looked out of his jacket and at the road ahead of us. I couldn't believe what I saw. Cars and trucks were driving toward us, then zipping past. Just before they'd get near, I'd tuck my head back inside Mr. James's jacket. I could feel the strong wind off each vehicle as it passed by. This crazy guy was going to get us killed! I tried my best to howl for help, but no one heard. I was stuffed too far down inside his jacket.

At least I had solved one mystery. Mr. James wore ski goggles, even though it was summertime, to protect his eyes. However, he wasn't protecting his eyes from snow blindness; there wasn't any snow. He wore them to protect his eyes from the dirt and debris kicked up by the tires  as cars raced by. We were sandblasted with every step. The jacket was getting hot, and I wanted to get some fresh air, but I had no idea how to tell Mr. James what I needed.

How would we ever become a family? He thought I was a pocket pet, and I thought he was crazy.

We were as different as a dog and a guy could possibly be.

CHAPTER FOUR

"Let's stop at a rest area."

I peeked out of his jacket to see what a rest area was. Did people take naps? Would there be a place for me to stretch out on my light-blue blanket? I wasn't sleepy, but I needed time to think.

I had prayed for a family and got a single guy. (And he wore ski goggles in the summer!)

I had prayed for a nice, fluffy bed and got stuffed inside a jacket.

I had prayed for a home and got the open highway.

Clearly I needed to have a long talk with God.

Peeking my head out, I saw green grass … as far as my eyes could see! I started squirming and whimpering, trying to get Mr. James's attention. I wanted to run! I had been dreaming of this moment. Maybe God had been listening after all.

Mr. James walked to a picnic table and shrugged off the Marmot bag he carried on his back. Then he stretched his legs and raised his arms over his head for another long stretch. Finally he reached inside his jacket, pulled me out, and set me down on the grass. The shadow from the picnic table made the grass cool and dark. I took my first step, feeling the little tickles of each blade of grass. It was soft! I made a mental note: *green feels soft*. Next, I sniffed it, my tail wagging.

Hmmm. So this is what green smells like.

I took a few more careful steps. This was the first time I'd ever set my paws on grass. I had dreamt of this moment so many times inside the shelter, looking out the window across the hall. All I ever dreamed of doing was running around and around in green grass.

So I did. I ran from one end of the rest area to the other, and then I ran in big, silly loops and back again. I ran past kids at a water fountain and barked at them to join me.

"The grass will feel so good on your paws!" I yelled. They were so far away that they didn't understand me, of course. No one ever really had. Sometimes I wondered if God did, either. But today … today was my day to run. Nothing was going to spoil that.

I zoomed past Mr. James. He laughed, watching me go.

He finished another round of stretching his legs, arms, and back. Then he called out to me. "Time to start walking again."

I didn't want to walk. I wanted to run. I pretended I didn't understand what Mr. James said. Of course dogs can understand every single word any human says. We usually pretend we don't, because sometimes people say terrible things, like "bath." There's just no reason to use language like that.

The real problem is that not everyone wants to listen to us. Every once in a while we hear of someone who does, but I had never met a person like that. The employees at the shelter said they didn't want to "get attached," but that makes no sense. It's a conversation, not superglue.

Mr. James called me again. "It's time to go. We need to start walking before the sun goes down."

He was making no sense. What did the sun have to do with running? I wasn't even tired.

I kept on running around, as fast as I could run. I barked for joy, wishing Parker and Stella could see me. I took another lap around the rest area for them.

Then Mr. James yelled, "It … is … time … to … go!" A few people turned their heads to stare at him. He cleared his throat and spoke in a softer voice. "Please, get over here, now."

I had heard him loud and clear. He had made sure of that.

Mr. James took a step toward me. I stopped. We made eye contact. Looking into his brown eyes, I knew two things: he was mad, and if I wanted to keep running, I had to be faster than him.

He made a fast dash and grab, but I shook him off and took off running again. *This is fun!*

Mr. James chased after me as I ran round and round, in circles and figure eights, just like Parker the Barker had done on the beach when the man chased after him.

I stopped running long enough for Mr. James to get near

me, and just when he'd get close enough to grab me, I took off again. I liked that game.

We ran for nearly an hour. Lots of people laughed.

Why wasn't Mr. James laughing?

"Stop! Stop!" He yelled that over and over. I did stop, many times. Then I started again. He didn't say that was against the rules.

I ran until there was a me-sized path worn into the green grass. Finally I was too tired to run anymore. I plopped down on my side. The cool grass tickled me all over. Mr. James's shoulders sagged, and he was breathing heavy. He slowly walked toward me. When he got closer, I gave him a big smile, wagging my tail.

Mr. James picked me up. He squinted at me with a frown on his face. After placing me inside his jacket, he walked back toward the highway, not saying anything. Inside the

jacket, I could hear his heart pounding. Maybe I had pushed him too far. Maybe he didn't like running as much as I did. He was so quiet. Mile after mile … silence.

Wait. Which direction are we walking? Were we going back toward the shelter? I started to panic.

"I'm sorry!" I howled. "I was only playing a game!"

Mr. James stopped. "Excuse me?" he said, looking around.

"I said I'm sorry," I repeated. "Please don't take me back. I promise to do better."

Mr. James scratched his head as another car zoomed by. There was no one walking on the road but us.

"Are you still mad at me?" I squeaked.

Finally, he looked straight down into his jacket, right at me. "Did you just say something?"

He wasn't just crazy; he was hard of hearing too!

"I said I'm sorry!" I yelled.

He lost his balance, rocking back on his feet. Then he yanked me out of his jacket, looked at me, and hugged me. My heart was racing now too.

"You can talk!" he said.

I knew he was being sarcastic, but not in a mean way. He was acting like this was the greatest news on earth.

"I can talk if you can listen," I said softly, not wanting to seem rude. We didn't know each other well enough yet to tease without hurting feelings. "Most anybody will talk if they're sure someone will listen."

"Oh, really?" he said. "Like when someone is calling your name over and over again, asking you to stop running?"

"I said I'm sorry," I whispered.

All of a sudden, he chuckled and softly patted me on my head. "All right, then. I guess I've done my fair share of talking. Now it's your turn, little girl. I'm listening."

"I just wanted to run. I didn't know it would make you so mad."

"I was afraid you were going to get injured by a car. Cars pull into the rest area really fast. People can be bad drivers when they're tired. That's why I got so upset with you." He cleared his throat and blinked several times. "But once I picked you up, all I could do was—"

"Was what?" I asked.

"All I could do was think about what that running must

have meant to you. It was the first time in your life you've been allowed out of your cage to run on the grass, am I right?"

I nodded.

He kissed the top of my head. "I'm so thankful I got to experience that moment with you."

This guy was full of surprises.

"Well, I'm still sorry, Mr. James," I said.

"It's okay. But do me a favor. Promise me you'll never run away from me like that again."

"Deal," I said. "Want to shake on it?"

"Sure." He stuck his hand out toward me.

I shook my body, hard, wiggling all the way down to the tip of my tail.

He just watched and laughed. Weird.

This guy had so much to learn.

CHAPTER FIVE

How many sunsets had I watched through the bars of my cage? Seeing the real thing was amazing. The afternoon sun dipped toward the horizon, and I kept my head out of the jacket, enjoying the view.

A green pickup truck pulled onto the side of the road. A lean cowboy wearing a dirt-stained white cowboy hat hollered out of his window. "Howdy! Are you that guy walking halfway across America for foster kids?"

"Yes sir, I am!"

"I'm his dog!" I added.

The guy chuckled and winked at me. "Hey there, cutie."

I wagged my tail. He had just called me cute!

He continued talking to Mr. James. "Well, me and my wife heard about you on the local news and wanted to invite you—and your little dog—to stay tonight in our farmhouse."

"That would be great!" Mr. James said.

"Hop on in the truck, and I'll take y'all to the house."

I braced myself. Mr. James didn't hop, though. He just walked.

Inside the pickup truck, the air smelled like sunshine and potato chips. I kind of liked it.

Mr. James sat me on his lap as the cowboy drove down the road.

"My name is Cowboy Costner."

"It's nice meeting you, Cowboy Costner. Thanks for inviting us to your farmhouse."

I sat quietly, listening to Mr. James and Cowboy Costner talk. They talked about the weather, oil prices, and politics.

Boring! If Parker were here, we'd hear some good stories.

We headed down the road in his Dodge pickup, past the windmills and cattle fields.

Mr. James didn't roll down the window, but there was so much dust on the road that I didn't complain. I wasn't sure if he'd let me borrow his goggles, anyway.

When we arrived at the farmhouse, Cowboy Costner's wife walked out the back door to meet us in the driveway. The screen door on their farmhouse smacked behind her. She had a kind soul. A dog can tell these things, you know.

"Hey, y'all! Welcome to our home. Come on in." She had a long Texas drawl. Texans loved to stretch out their words, maybe so they'd have something to fill up all those open spaces with.

"Thank you, ma'am," Mr. James said.

Cowboy Costner held the door open for us, and we followed Mrs. Costner inside the farmhouse. Mr. James was carrying me in one arm, so I got a good look around at the place. There was lots of antique furniture and many little whatnots. Some of them shared an odd shape, like a barrel with a broom handle sticking out of it.

"You collect butter churns?" Mr. James asked.

"Yes! I have for many years," she replied, reaching out to pat me on the head. "You're just big enough to fit inside one," she said. I think she meant it as a joke, but I ducked my head. I didn't know what a butter churn was, but I did not want to find out.

She led us past the staircase and grandfather clock and to a guest room down the hallway. "Here's where y'all will be sleeping tonight. Towels are in the bathroom closet. Make yourselves at home," she said.

Mr. James set his backpack down on the floor and then sat down in the rocking chair in the room. "It sure feels good to rest my feet."

I kept my head ducked down. This was the first house I had ever set paws in. Sometimes when you dream of something your whole life, you feel scared when it actually happens. Even if you don't know why.

He stroked the fur along my back. "You probably think I'm crazy for staying in a complete stranger's home, don't you?"

That's exactly what I was thinking, but who was I to accuse him of being crazy? After all, I was the one who left the shelter with a shaggy-haired, scruffy-faced stranger wearing goggles on his head. At least the cowboy and his wife didn't *look* crazy.

Mr. James explained that he'd been staying in a different stranger's home just about every day since the walk began in Nashville.

"People hear on the radio about 'the guy walking halfway across America,' or they read about me in the newspaper or see me on the news, and they want to help. So they find me alongside the road and offer me a room in their home for the night. Then that person tells someone they know in the next town and that person does the same thing. There are some really good people in this world."

I thought about the big black door back at the shelter. "Did you ever meet anyone along the way who wasn't nice?"

"Of course I did." He settled back into the chair, and I knew a story was coming. "When I walked out of Nashville on January 1, 2010, it was about 7 degrees. The wind chill was about fifteen below zero. An arctic blast had moved in during the night. I'd already walked through Memphis, St. Francis County, and Little Rock, Arkansas. I had never been so cold, or so grateful for my warm clothes and sleeping bag."

I nodded, even though I'd never heard of those places and had no idea what a sleeping bag was.

"I was just outside of Hot Springs when someone robbed me. Took all of my warm clothes and my backpack. The only thing they allowed me to keep was what I had on."

I gasped. "Someone robbed you? But you're trying to help foster kids!" I tucked my tail between my legs, picturing the bad guy.

"Snow was pelting me and the ice was blowing sideways. Ice hurts when it hits you like that." He rubbed his hands along his arms, the memory making him cold.

"Were you scared?"

"Sure. Then a man driving on Highway 8 saw me walking along the shoulder of the road. He pulled over his truck and asked me why I was walking and where I was going. I explained who I was and what I was doing. I told him I'd been robbed. He couldn't believe that had happened, right in his town! He invited me to come back to his ranch and stay on his ranch until my friends at Marmot could ship me some new clothes."

I cocked my head to the side. "Marmot?"

"That's the company that sent me supplies and equipment. I couldn't do this alone."

I nodded, then rested my head again.

"So … I hopped into his warm truck, and we headed to the Pea Patch Ranch. He turned onto a road, marked by a hubcap hanging on a fence post, then drove up a long dirt road. There was a wooden fence separating the dirt road from a big field with lots of cows in it. Roosters and hens scattered when we drove up to the house with a tin roof. I wondered why they didn't want to get inside and get warm. Especially when I found out what was waiting for me inside that ol' house."

I perked up. "What was it?"

"Food! I remember how that spring on the screen door squeaked loudly as we walked inside, and how I had never been so happy to get out of a storm. I could smell the cornbread already baking and stew simmering on the stovetop. He and his wife fed me, and I met their dog, Max. He was such a good dog. You would have liked him a lot. I watched as he helped wrangle up all the cattle in the field when it was time to feed them."

He sounded amazing.

"A few days later, I finally received the package from Marmot with new clothes and a backpack in it. I packed up and said good-bye to the good folks on the Pea Patch Ranch."

"Wow! Those people saved your life. You could have frozen to death."

"It just goes to show that the world isn't all bad."

I relaxed, glad to know this wasn't a story about serial killers.

"I didn't want to leave because the ranch was so cozy and the couple was so nice, but I had to keep walking."

I wondered how far he still had left to walk. Would it be rude to ask? I didn't want to seem ungrateful. I still wasn't even sure why he had chosen me for adoption.

"I met more wonderful people in Mena, Arkansas, at the Friendship House Coffee Shoppe. The owner paid for my cup of coffee. It warmed my hands and my heart. I've learned that there are a lot of good people in the world."

"Well … as long as you're not afraid to stay here, then I'm not afraid to stay here," I said.

"You have absolutely nothing to worry about. I will be right here to protect you at all times. But these folks are very nice, and I believe they just want to do something good. Just like I'm trying to do something good, just like the folks on the Pea Patch Ranch were trying to do something good. Helping people is contagious, you know," Mr. James said with a grin.

I looked down at my paws. Contagious? I wasn't sure I wanted to catch anything. Except for a few winks of sleep.

CHAPTER SIX

"I sure do appreciate the hospitality you and your lovely wife shared with me and my little dog here," Mr. James said over the early breakfast Mrs. Costner had prepared.

Cowboy Costner smiled. "It was our pleasure. It was the least we could do to show our appreciation for someone who's doing something good for someone else."

After everyone had stuffed themselves, including me, Cowboy Costner drove us to the exact spot where he picked us up the day before.

Mr. James opened the truck door and stepped out on the gravel ground. He reached into the bed of the truck, taking his backpack and trekking poles. My stomach did a little flip. Was he going to leave me?

Next, he picked me up off the front seat and put me inside his jacket. I breathed a sigh of relief.

"Oh, that reminds me!" Mr. Costner reached under the seat. "Mrs. Costner made up a little goodie bag for your dog. There are a few treats in there along with food. I'm sure she'll enjoy it."

I could feel my eyes getting big like the Texas morning sun. I could not wait to see what was in the goodie bag. I licked my lips, ready to dig in. It's never too early for a second breakfast!

Instead of feeding me, Mr. James took the bag and put it inside his fanny pack with all the loose change he'd been collecting along the roadside.

Grrrr.

Cowboy Costner tipped his cowboy hat and drove away.

"I need to find a pet store," Mr. James said.

My stomach did a big flip again. *Was he going to sell me? Is that why he chosen me?* "What for?" I squeaked out.

"To buy a leash, so you can walk beside me." He reached up and scratched me between my ears. That made me feel better.

"I would love to walk beside you, Mr. James. I don't need a leash. I promise not to run away."

To my surprise, Mr. James set me down on the ground right then.

"Mr. James, aren't you afraid I'm going to run?"

"You promised you wouldn't run, and I trust you. If you do run, then I'll know you're dishonest, and I won't be able to trust you again."

That sounded so … final. "Is it really that important to be honest?" I asked.

"Dishonesty gives you a bad reputation. If you get a bad reputation, then no one will trust you. Plus, it compromises your integrity."

"Integrity and reputation sound like the same thing to me."

"They're not the same thing." He stopped walking and looked at me. I could tell he thought this was important. "Integrity is who you are, and reputation is who people think you are."

I cocked my head to one side, thinking about that.

He continued. "Let's say John Doe has a reputation for being a good guy. He makes promises to the public, and they believed him. They think he's an honest guy. But the public catches him in a lie. People realized, too late, that he has no integrity. Now no one wants to be associated with him, because he has a bad reputation. See how those two are connected?"

I wagged my tail briefly, thinking. I needed to stay right by his side and prove I had good integrity.

As we walked past tall silos and old barns and dogs that barked behind their fenced-in yards, I never left Mr. James's side. Not even when the sun went down and the shadows grew long.

We finally reached Amarillo, Texas. Amarillo is the halfway point between Nashville, Tennessee, and Phoenix, Arizona, Mr. James said. There were lots of people waiting in a music store parking lot to meet him when he arrived. Several of them carried posters and handmade signs to cheer him on. When the first guy introduced himself, he said that most everyone there was a foster parent or foster child.

Mr. James grabbed a permanent marker out of his bag and started signing autographs.

I got a good look at the kids standing around. Why were they in foster care? They all looked like good kids. They smiled and petted me. One girl said I had the most beautiful underbite she'd ever seen. These kids were smart too.

Why had someone let them go?

Maybe for the same reason someone had let me go.

Mr. James posed for lots of photos with the crowd and thanked all of them for coming out and showing their support. He seemed comfortable with everyone. I wondered if he had ever been nervous around people. If he ever had, I sure couldn't tell. He probably had been one of those guys who had rich parents and lots of friends and didn't have a clue how hard life was for anyone else. I licked him on the cheek anyway. I didn't want to be mad at him for being lucky.

After the celebration, we went to a Mexican restaurant. A mariachi band serenaded guests from the porch. Their music flooded my heart with sunshine-happiness. Even their costumes made me happy: sombreros with matching outfits filled with gold-thread embroidery and beading.

All the musicians waved at me and petted my head as we walked by and into the restaurant. I decided I liked mariachi bands very much.

CHAPTER SEVEN

It was much cooler inside the restaurant. I sighed and stretched, happy to feel the cold air. The interior walls were lime green and boasted hand-painted murals. One was of a man sitting on a horse, looking at a woman standing in a window. He looked exactly like the man playing the ukulele in the mariachi band.

Inside the restaurant was an explosion of color: big silver pinwheels hung on the walls, paper flowers in vases sat on painted wooden chairs and tables, punched tin sconces and star-shaped lights were strung from the red ceiling. The whole place screamed *party*.

Mr. James tucked me under his jacket as the hostess led us to a table in the corner. Guessing that dogs weren't allowed in this place, I kept as still and quiet as I could.

A gentleman set a basket of tortilla chips and a bowl of salsa on the table. Mr. James said a blessing, thanking God for our food, and then dropped a few tortilla chips inside his jacket for me.

They crunched when I bit into them, so even though I was really hungry, I took little nibbles and chewed quickly. Mr. James started laughing, and people stared, no doubt wondering what was so funny. He didn't seem embarrassed. But I was.

When he dropped a chip near me, I grabbed it. I was so hungry I forgot to chew with my mouth closed.

Mr. James whipped his head left, then right. He had heard the loud crunching sound, I was sure of it. He must have wanted people to think it had come from another table.

A few seconds later, I took another bite. This time I chewed faster and the sound was even louder.

He looked around again, then looked inside his jacket. "You're going to get us in trouble," he whispered. "Can you eat a little quieter?"

I tried. But there's no way to eat a tortilla chip quietly. I crunched, but Mr. James crunched louder, trying to drown out my crunch. I crunched again. Then Mr. James crunched even louder. People at the table beside us glared at Mr. James. I could tell they thought he had terrible manners.

Mr. James looked inside his jacket again. "You are going

to get us in trouble if you keep crunching that loud."

He caught me mid-crunch. I stared at him, and he stared at me, until I saw him struggling not to laugh.

"You're just worried I can out-crunch you," I said.

"No one can out-crunch a country boy."

Now, instead of quieting our crunches, we crunched even louder.

Before we'd even finished the basket of chips, the table

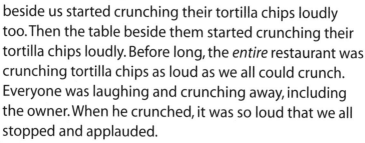

beside us started crunching their tortilla chips loudly too. Then the table beside them started crunching their tortilla chips loudly. Before long, the *entire* restaurant was crunching tortilla chips as loud as we all could crunch. Everyone was laughing and crunching away, including the owner. When he crunched, it was so loud that we all stopped and applauded.

The mariachi band came inside to see what all the commotion was. They tried crunching tortilla chips as loudly as they could too. Family members tried to out-crunch one another. It was sisters against brothers, moms against dads, grandpas against grandmas. One old lady dug into

her bag, pulled out her teeth, and popped them in, then crunched away. Everyone crunched until there were no tortilla chips left in the entire restaurant.

After we left, we didn't talk for a while. I think Mr. James needed time to digest all the chips he had eaten.

"What a party that was," he said finally. "It all started with you, pup. If you hadn't crunched a tortilla chip loudly, there wouldn't have been a party at all."

"I only crunch so loudly because of my underbite. Is that cheating?"

"No. Maybe that's why God gave you an underbite, so you could help people have a little fun. Those families were sitting around ignoring one another, playing on their cell phones, not talking. Thanks to you and your underbite, they enjoyed a little family time. More than likely, they needed it. Looked to me like they'd been taking each other for granted for a very long time. You brought them back together. Great job, pup. I'm so proud of you."

I was proud of me too.

And for the record, I out-crunched Mr. James.

We had been walking for about an hour after the crunch contest when Mr. James stopped and checked his map. "We've got to walk at least fifteen miles today."

I settled down into his jacket, happy to watch the scenery while he did all the walking.

"The guidebook says we're on historic Route 66."

Rusted hotel signs, old fuel pumps, and cars sitting in front of old buildings caught my attention. I wondered why so many places were empty and deserted.

"This is a very famous road," Mr. James said. "A famous American writer, John Steinbeck, referred to it as The

Mother Road in his book *The Grapes of Wrath*. Wow, was that a great story!" He looked around, shaking his head. "I can hardly believe we're walking on the exact road he wrote about."

Why would a writer put this road in a book? I didn't get it. Still, Mr. James seemed very impressed.

"Route 66 starts in Chicago," he continued, "and ends at the Santa Monica Pier in California. That's a little over twenty-five hundred miles."

I wasn't sure how far twenty-five hundred miles was. I just wanted to do my fifteen for the day and relax.

My eyelids got heavy.

Mr. James piped up again.

"Now, it's a hundred fifty miles from the shelter to here. Just imagine walking that distance seventeen times."

I panicked. Was he changing his mind about taking me such a long distance? Did he know how weird I thought it was that he used poles to help him walk? Or how weird I thought he was because he brushed his teeth every night, even if I told him his breath had the perfect amount of stink?

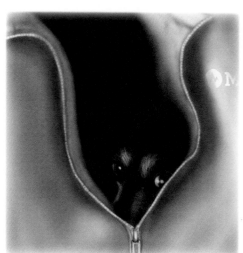

"That's not far," I said, trying to sound hopeful.

He scoffed. "It's not far when someone is carrying you."

I pulled my head back inside Mr. James's jacket. I was weighing him down.

"Oh, I'm sorry, little girl," he quickly added.

"I'm not complaining; I'm explaining. I like carrying you. Plus you only weigh five pounds."

I refused to poke my head back out.

"Aw, c'mon, pup! I'm only trying to give you some perspective of how far twenty-five hundred miles is." He dug around in his bag and offered me one of Mrs. Costner's doggie treats. That was worth poking my head out for. However, I still didn't say anything. I wasn't mad. I was worried.

Did Mr. James regret adopting me? I was extra weight.

As the afternoon wore on, Mr. James snapped a few photos of the old buildings and signs. As he walked, he hummed a little song. Suddenly he stopped, grabbed his phone, and hummed a few notes into it.

"Why are you doing that?" I asked.

"I'm recording a melody, so I won't forget it later."

"A melody? What's that?"

"It's a musical idea for a song. Songs have to start somewhere. Sometimes they start with words and other times they start with a melody. On a good day a song will start with a melody and words at the same time."

"Is this a good day?" I asked.

Mr. James didn't answer. He kept humming into his phone, and his eyes had a faraway look.

NAT KING COLE
PERFORMING LIVE

THIS FRIDAY AT

Vittles
RESTAURANT

CHAPTER EIGHT

Suddenly Mr. James stopped humming and poked me. He pointed to the road at our feet. "A songwriter and pianist by the name of Bobby Troupe was inspired by this very road we're on and wrote a song called 'Get Your Kicks on Route 66.' A singer named Nat King Cole recorded it."

He sang part of the song for me. I wagged my tail to the rhythm.

"This road has inspired so many people, pup. There was even a man by the name of Andy Payne who led the first and only foot race from Los Angeles to Chicago in 1928 on this road."

I looked down at the road. It just looked like a road. I wasn't inspired at all.

Why did anyone care about a road? Was Mr. James trying to distract me? Maybe he still wished for a different dog, a dog who liked talking about roads.

Mr. James cleared his throat, so I knew he was getting ready to try to teach me something. "President Eisenhower decided America needed a bigger and better highway. He wanted one with more lanes to transport military vehicles and machinery faster, especially during wartime. So he built a new road, one called a 'Super Highway.'"

Mr. James went on and on about the road. My eyelids grew heavy.

"When the Super Highway was born, Route 66 died. Although 80 percent of it is still drivable, it's become more of a sidewalk than a business route. Eisenhower may have protected America from the outside, but a different enemy won from the inside." He shook his head.

I looked around, but there were no signs of any enemy. I got up the courage to ask the question that had been tugging on my heart. "Mr. James, do you regret adopting me? Will I be like this old road? You're okay for now, but one day you'll find another dog you like better?"

Mr. James stopped walking. "What? Are you kidding me?

Why, no! I mean … absolutely not. Never! What made you ask that question?"

"I'm afraid you're going to give me away."

"I'll never give you away. You are my friend and I am yours, through thick and thin. I will always be right here by your side, no matter what."

I wanted to believe Mr. James. He probably wanted to believe it himself. But I knew something he didn't: not everyone means it when they say "forever." Life in the shelter taught me that.

He reached up to scratch behind my ears, and I licked his hand.

🐾

We walked past the Cadillac Ranch. Most ranches have cows, chickens, and tractors. And barns with spider webs hanging in the corners that look like big, round vinyl records.

This ranch had ten Cadillacs half-buried nose-first in the ground. The ten Cadillacs formed a single-file line, looking as if they had driven off the edge of heaven, fallen to earth, and stuck in the ground.

I used my paw to tap Mr. James's head. "Why are those cars sticking out of the ground?" I asked.

"It's a monument built by the Ant Farm," Mr. James said.

"Wow!" I whistled in admiration. "That must have taken billions of ants to carry each one of those cars, dig those holes, and put a Cadillac in each one." Those were some amazing ants.

Mr. James laughed. "Ants didn't do that. A group of hippies from San Francisco, who called themselves Ant Farm, made this. They traveled here in 1974 and put the Cadillacs in the holes."

"Why would anyone call themselves an ant farm?"

Mr. James shrugged. "Why would anyone stick Cadillacs in the ground?"

"Good point."

"Over the decades, the cars have been stripped and splattered with a variety of Day-Glo paints. People come from all over the world to see the Cadillac Ranch."

"Just to see cars sticking out of the ground?"

"Well, small things entertain small minds." He sighed. "But it's also a great reminder that the things that mean the most aren't things at all."

"Huh?"

"Those cars used to be a symbol of wealth and prosperity. Everyone wanted cars just like those. Now they're just ten old, rusted, battered frames stuck in the ground. The only value they have is to warn us not to value things more than people."

I looked at Mr. James, with his fanny pack and backpack. He didn't have a lot of stuff. "What do you value, Mr. James?"

"I value opportunities. I want to laugh and learn. I value the sunshine, rain, parks, and animals. I value time, and spending it with people I love, and making lifelong memories."

"I wish I had someone to love."

"What am I, chopped liver?" Mr. James said.

"I wish you were. I'm hungry."

He laughed and grabbed another treat out of his bag.

"What does it feel like to love someone?" I asked in between bites.

"When you care so much for another person's heart that you want to be completely unselfish … that's love. It's something you feel *and* something you do."

We continued walking along Route 66 toward the setting sun. It was late evening, and the sky was beautiful.

"Look at that horizon. It's ruby-red," he said. Suddenly he stopped. "That's it!"

"What's it?" I asked.

"I'd like to name you Ruby, if that's okay with you."

"Ruby is fine with me. It's better than a number."

"Okay, then, Ruby it is." He grabbed a permanent marker

out of his fanny pack, the same marker he used for giving autographs. He took off my collar before setting me on the ground. Holding my tag in one hand, he crossed out the number 127 and wrote RUBY in big letters. He held it out for me to inspect. I nodded my approval and barked.

I finally had a name. I liked it too. Maybe he wasn't going to give me away after all.

But someone gave this road a name and later abandoned it. And somewhere out in the world, I had a mom who had given birth to me and then, I guess, she didn't want me anymore.

I sighed, trying not to let Mr. James know how scared I felt. I didn't understand it, either. The closer we became as friends, the more he insisted we were family, the more I began to realize how bad it would hurt when he left.

CHAPTER NINE

The ruby-red sky faded to darkest blue. That color matched my heart. My thoughts were tangled and ugly. I wanted to turn off my feelings, but I didn't know how.

Why am I walking down the side of an abandoned road with a man wearing ski goggles? Why am I not with a normal family with a normal house and a normal yard? Maybe I should run away the next time Mr. James sets me down. At least I wouldn't have to worry about being abandoned. If I leave Mr. James instead, that would hurt less, wouldn't it?

Mr. James set me down a few times, but I couldn't run away, not without my blue towel. That was the only thing I owned.

This is going to take some planning.

He picked me up, stuck me back in his jacket, and walked on as if everything was fine and dandy.

"You okay in there?"

"I'm okay." That was the truth, but it wasn't the whole truth. I was only okay for now. I needed to get away from Mr. James so he wouldn't break my heart when he left me.

The following morning Mr. James tried for several hours to walk against the strong headwind in Vega, Texas. It was impossible, so he decided to stop and rest for the day.

The wind wasn't nearly as bad the next day.

After walking twenty miles, Mr. James found an area off the side of Route 66 where he could pitch a tent. He swept the ground around the sagebrush with his shoe to make sure there were no rocks that would poke through the tent floor. As Mr. James built a small fire and unpacked the tent, I decided it was time to make a run for it.

One. Two. I took a few deep breaths. *You can do this,* I kept saying to myself. *Just go!*

Mr. James hummed as he put up the tent.

I ran as hard and fast as I could, through the trees, shrubs, and behind a very small building. I hid behind a pile of wood.

"Ruby! Ruby!"

I could hear Mr. James calling my name, but he couldn't see me.

"Ruby! Ruuuuuuuuuby! Please come back."

I remained in one spot and didn't move.

Mr. James walked around and around, calling out my name over and over. I could tell he was scared. Was his heart breaking too? Because mine was. Running away hurt worse than staying. How could I have been so stupid?

"Oh, please, Ruby, come back."

Pushing my paw through the logs, I made a little hole to watch.

Finally he saw me. His eyes got big. "Ruby! There you are."

I tucked my tail and dropped my head. Would he be angry? Would he understand?

"Ruby, sweetie, what happened?"

I shook my head, not answering.

"Did I say something or do something that startled you?" he asked. "Why are you so afraid?"

I had to take a big breath to get the words out, because they were stuck way down inside my heart. "Mr. James, I'm afraid you're going to abandon me, so I ran away before you had a chance to."

"Ruby, I understand."

"You do?" Now my eyes got big.

He nodded. "You wanted to leave me before I could leave you so it wouldn't hurt as bad. Right?"

I nodded, my eyes not meeting his.

"Ruby, I know I've already said this before, but I'll *never* leave you. You are stuck with me."

A tear slid down my cheek.

Mr. James petted my head. "It takes time to let your feelings catch up to your new life. I know."

I wanted to be stuck together. I wanted to *feel* stuck together. Now I had made a mess of things.

Mr. James could probably tell that I was still upset. "Ruby," he said, "I want you to repeat these words: I'm important. I'm smart. I'm strong. And I'm beautiful." He tapped his foot, waiting.

"Right now, you mean?" I asked.

He nodded.

I felt silly, but I repeated every word. "I'm important. I'm smart. I'm strong. And I'm beautiful."

He smiled, but not the kind of smile when someone thinks you're funny. I think he was smiling because he was proud of me. But I still had one worry.

"Is my integrity bad now?" I asked. "Do I have a bad reputation?"

"No, Ruby. There's a big difference between doing a

bad thing and running for your life because you're afraid someone is going to abandon you. You were just protecting yourself. I get it. That's how I feel with God sometimes. Sometimes I want to reject Him when I'm in pain or afraid. I want to run away. But you know what? He knows our hearts and minds and shows us mercy and grace."

He wiped the tear off my cheek then gave me a big, sweet kiss right on top of my head. "That's exactly what I'm going to do with you too. Now, let's go on back to the tent and settle in for the night. You never know what kind of red-eyed wolves are out this time of the evening."

"Mr. James!" I yelled. "I was just starting to relax! Don't talk about red-eyed wolves!"

He laughed as he stood up and motioned for me to follow.

And you know what? I did. I followed real close, and not just because I was scared of red-eyed wolves. I used to think Mr. James had a lot to learn. But so did I.

Mr. James and I lay inside the Marmot tent, listening to the sounds of the night. I lay on my light-blue towel as we stared through the screened roof at the bright stars hanging in that beautiful Adrian sky.

A coyote howled in the distance. He sure sounded lonely. But there was no way I was sharing my blanket. I stretched out, trying to cover every possible inch of it, just in case Mr. James got any ideas.

Crickets rubbed their wings together, making chirping sounds.

Mr. James sighed. "Ruby, three months ago I was sleeping on a fancy tour bus. I have to admit, it was much more comfortable than this ground we're lying on."

"What's a tour bus?"

"It's a rectangular-shaped home that rolls on wheels, with a driver. It looks like a school bus on the outside, but it doesn't look or feel anything like a school bus on the inside."

"Is it like a shelter?"

"It's more like a mobile home. It has a living room, kitchen, bathroom, and sleeping area. It also has a TV, air-conditioning, and heat. Musicians, like the Mariachi band we saw at the Mexican restaurant, live on tour buses and ride from one venue to the next, performing concerts in front of thousands of people."

"Why did you travel on a tour bus with musicians?" I asked. "Wait a minute! Were you in a mariachi band?"

"No, Ruby, I'm a country music singer." He held out his hands and I studied them. "See how long my nails are? That's because I play guitar too. I use my long nails to help me pluck the strings. And when I performed concerts with my band, the Black Elbow Boys, at places like Madison Square Garden, Red Rocks, and on the *Grand Ole Opry* show, we'd travel by tour bus."

"What country is your music from?"

"That's the funniest thing I've ever heard, Ruby." Mr. James laughed. "Country music is not music from another country; it's a genre of music. Country musicians play certain instruments to create a special sound. That sound represents where the music originated, which is the southern United States. The instruments include a banjo, fiddle, steel guitar, drums, bass guitar, acoustic guitar, and a singer."

"So it is from a country. It's from this country," I said.

"Well, you're right, Ruby. And you're smart."

"Thanks."

"But it's not just one particular sound. Country music has evolved a lot since the 1920s, when it originated."

I held up a paw to interrupt him. "What does Black Elbow Boys mean?"

"My friends and I used to work on our old cars like those Cadillacs back at the Cadillac Ranch. Grease from the engines would get on our tools. Then we'd set the tools down on the front fenders of the cars. Grease would get on the fenders, and when we'd rest our elbows on the fenders, grease would get on our elbows and turn them black. I thought Black Elbow Boys would be a cool name for a country band since the music represents hard-working, blue-collar people. Those people can relate to working on old cars like we did."

"Why didn't you wash your elbows? You could be the Clean Elbow Boys."

"We did wash our elbows!" He laughed. "But the name stuck, just like grease on your elbows."

I had no clue what Madison Square Garden, Red Rocks, or the *Opry* was, but I couldn't imagine Mr. James was really a country singer. At the shelter, Ms. Valory had worn a T-shirt with a country singer on it. That guy had tattoos on his neck, plus he wore a ball cap over his shaved head, and he wore earrings. He looked like he spent a lot of time looking in the mirror.

I licked my paw and tried to smooth back Mr. James's hair. It didn't budge. His hair was thick. I spat in my paw and tried again.

"What are you doing?" Mr. James hollered.

"Trying to make you look like a singer. You're too scruffy."

CHAPTER TEN

Mr. James pushed my paw away.

I groaned. "Listen, I know about these things!" I gave him my most serious look. "People always judge by appearances."

"But Ruby, things aren't always what they appear to be. For example, one time there was a ball sitting in my neighbor's yard. A few of the guys and I were standing around one of the old cars we'd been working on. One of the guys said, 'Fellers, see that ball? I'm going to run as fast as I can and kick that ball out of this neighborhood.'

"All the guys were laughing and cheering him on. The runner took off his flip-flops and sprinted across the yard as fast as he could run. We were all cheering and chanting his name and saying 'Go! Go!' When he neared the ball, he reared back and kicked it as hard as he could. But it didn't move."

"What?" I frowned. "Why not?"

"It was a bowling ball. The guy fell on the ground, screaming and holding his foot. His foot had already started to swell up, too, because it was broken. The moral of the story? You can't judge something or someone by the way they look."

I shrugged. "People did that every day at the shelter."

"Yeah, I know," Mr. James said, winking at me. "And just think of what they missed."

"Where is the *Grand Ole Opry*?" I asked. "Will we see it on our walk?"

"The *Grand Ole Opry* isn't a place. It's a radio show broadcast from the Opry House every Saturday night. Sometimes, though, they broadcast from the Ryman Auditorium. The Ryman Auditorium is an old church with stained-glass windows, and the audience sits on church pews. The Opry House is a bigger version of the Ryman Auditorium.

"So, two places?" I asked.

He nodded.

"The radio show started on November 28, 1925, and was originally called *Old Time Tunes*. Then it became *The WSM Barn Dance* shortly afterwards. A general manager from Chicago named George Hay invited a fiddle player named Uncle Jimmy Thompson to perform on the show. It was the first time someone played an instrument on the show. It was a huge success, so other fiddle and harmonica players performed on the show. The music sounded exactly like the music from rural Tennessee. The audience loved it!"

"Fiddle and harmonica?" I scratched my neck. "That doesn't sound like an opera."

"It's not an opera at all." Mr. James laughed. "In 1927, George joked by calling the radio show a 'grand opera' because it came on after a classical music show. The name *Grand Ole Opry* stuck. Since 1925, thousands of musicians and singers have performed on the *Grand Ole Opry* show. It is the longest-running live radio program in the world. It's the show that made country music famous."

"Is that why you record melodies on your phone?" I asked. "Are you writing songs to sing on the *Grand Ole Opry*?"

"That's my plan, Ruby. But I can't play just any old song on the *Opry*. I have to play a *great* song. And in order to play a great song, I have to write one. Or find one."

"How do you find songs? Is it like finding coins on the side of the road?"

"I wish it were that easy," Mr. James said, shaking his head. "When I first moved to Nashville, a thousand songs were being written every day on Music Row. Music Row is the heart of Nashville, the place where all great songs are written. After a song is written, a music publisher publishes it. If a singer likes a particular song, he or she will license that song from the publisher, then record it, and—"

"Whoa!" I interrupted. "A song has to go from your phone, to Nashville, to a publisher, and then to a recording studio? How do you know if a song is worth all that trouble?"

"I just have to trust." Mr. James sighed. "And I have to be ready. Writing a song starts with an idea. I never know where the idea will come from. Things I see, hear, feel, or even taste inspire me. An idea might start as just a few words or with a melody, like the melodies I've been recording into my phone. Sometimes I write the song by myself. Other times I share the words and melody with another songwriter."

I glanced at my blue blanket. "I don't like sharing."

He laughed. "It's always good to have a second opinion. The two of us might sit in a room with one of us playing guitar and the other playing piano. Or we might not play any instruments at all. We'll share words and melodies. Sometimes we agree on what each other shares, other times we don't. This process can go on for hours. Eventually, hopefully, after talking and singing back and forth, piecing words and melodies together, we end up with a great song. It sounds easier than it is. I've written songs within thirty minutes and others have taken years to write."

"Why do you work so hard to write songs? Why don't you do something easier?"

"This is how God made me, Ruby. But I'll tell you a secret I've learned about the music business."

I leaned in, curious.

"The most important thing to remember about songwriting is that 'the bottom holds up the top.' In other words, everyone in the whole music industry had to start at the same place: with a song. No one becomes a superstar without a song."

"Will you write a song about me, Mr. James?"

"Ha-ha! That's mighty forward of you. What makes you think you deserve a song written about you?"

"I'm cute! I can help you write it too. You probably don't know all the cute things about me yet."

"Oh, really? Well, I'll think about it."

We were quiet for a few minutes, then I asked one more question. "Mr. James, if you're a country singer, then why are you walking halfway across America for foster children?"

He got very quiet. I wondered if I had said something wrong. Why did I always ask so many questions?

Mr. James must have noticed that I was worried, because suddenly, he gave me a big smile. "Ruby, when I was a young boy, about fourteen years old, I'd listen to music through my earphones and pretend I was that person on stage singing. I'd sing along with their music and dream of being a star someday. You have to imagine your dream coming true, and then believe it can. After years of hard work, my dream finally came true. I had songs on the radio and many fans who would listen to my music through their earphones. It was like everything had come full circle."

"Like chasing your tail!" I interrupted.

"No, Ruby! Like my dream had come true, and now I was inspiring other kids. Then one night, while I was on stage at Madison Square Garden looking out at eighteen thousand screaming fans, God spoke to me."

"God came to your show?" I hollered. That was the coolest thing I had ever heard.

Mr. James stared at me, one eyebrow raised. I gulped and put a paw over my mouth.

"Ruby, God speaks to us in our hearts. That's what I meant. Anyway, I heard God say, 'A real star shines so others can find their way.' In other words, I had to do more with my talent than just entertain people. I had to use my resources to help others. I decided to turn the spotlight on foster kids.

I decided to walk halfway across America to raise awareness for the thirty thousand who age out each year in America and become homeless."

"Age out?" I cocked my head. I'd never heard that expression before.

"When foster kids turn eighteen, they are no longer eligible for care. They often become homeless."

"Oh, no!" I couldn't imagine that. "No family? No home?"

"No. Those kids are all alone." He shook his head. "I want to change that."

I nodded.

"So on New Year's Day in 2010, I walked out of Nashville and headed for Phoenix, Arizona, which is halfway across America. My record label and all my friends cheered me on as I walked out of the city that day. They knew I'd be back in three months to start touring again."

"Wow! Were you nervous?"

He shrugged. "I think I probably felt the same way that Noah felt when God told him to use his talents to build an ark. Did you know that it had never rained on earth before? Noah didn't know what rain was, or what a flood was, or why he would ever need an ark. But Noah trusted God and was obedient, even when everyone made fun of him. After he built the ark, it rained forty days and forty nights and flooded the earth. Noah saved his family and two of each animal on earth, and they were the only ones who survived. I knew I was going to be okay, too, as long as I trusted God."

"What happened to the animals that didn't get to go on the ark? Do you think they became part of the carousel ride in Central Park?"

"What? No. The carousel animals aren't real. Did you think they were petrified?"

I nodded, and he started laughing. "It's not funny, Mr. James! What happened to all those other animals?"

"I believe God provided a special escape route during the great flood, and they all went to heaven where they are safe and sound."

"Maybe they became angels who watch over us every day," I added.

"If so, we'd better be good to all the animals on earth," Mr. James added. "Especially if some of them could be angels."

I waited for him to ask if I was an angel. He didn't. Mr. James was hard to train, I guess. I batted my eyelashes and wagged my tail. He just kept staring up at the stars. Finally, I changed the subject. "So there were storms back then too?"

"Yes, Ruby, there were storms back then. Unfortunately, there will always be storms. But if we didn't have storms, we wouldn't appreciate the sunshine."

"I love the sunshine. I love how it feels on my face. It makes me happy."

"The sunshine is like a smile. It's good to feel the warmth, but that's not enough. We have to shine for others so they can feel it too. Who knows? They could be going through storms in their lives, and your smile might cheer them up. You might help them get through the storm."

I liked that idea. But surely I could do more to help people than just smile. "Mr. James, do I have a talent?"

"Everyone has a talent, Ruby. No matter who we are or where we come from, we all have talents. You may not know what your talent is, but there's absolutely no doubt you have one."

"I bet my talent is running."

"Not without a leash, it isn't." Mr. James laughed. He thought that was funny.

I squinted at him, trying to look tough. "I don't need a leash to run fast."

"I know you don't, Ruby, but you do need a big yard, or a safe place to run, far away from vehicles."

"When we get back to your house in Nashville, will I have a big yard?"

"Yes." Mr. James yawned. "But for now, say your bedtime prayers and let's see which one of us is *talented* enough to fall asleep within the next thirty seconds."

"Okay. Good night, Mr. James."

"Good. Night. Ruby!"

One, two, three, four, five, six, seven, eight, nine, ten, eleven—

"Mr. James?"

"Yes, Ruby?"

"Did I win?"

"Not yet. Be quiet and keep trying."

I whined.

Mr. James sighed. "Good night, Ruby." He sounded aggravated, so I waited a moment before telling him the bad news.

"I've got to potty."

Mr. James sighed. "Is it an emergency?"

"That depends."

"That depends on what?" he asked.

"How dry you like your blankets."

He grabbed a flashlight and unzipped the tent. He must really like dry blankets.

Famous people can be so picky.

CHAPTER ELEVEN

The following morning, Mr. James watched the sun come up and sipped instant coffee from a tin cup that he kept attached to his backpack. He stood and stretched.

"Ruby, I need to go down to the stream and wash up. Can you wait inside the tent until I come back?"

"Last night you said you would never leave me."

"I'm not leaving," he said. "I'm taking a bath. That's different."

"I don't want a bath."

"I didn't say you had to take one. I do. Now, I'm just going over the hill and down to the stream. It'll take me about twenty minutes. Then I'll come right back."

Mr. James walked away. I watched as his gray Marmot hat disappeared over the edge of the riverbank. I waited. After a few minutes, there was no sign of Mr. James. I was nervous. Mr. James had promised he would be right back.

The coyote howled, sounding much closer than last night. I paced around inside the tent. Mr. James didn't have anything I could use to defend myself. Except his stinky socks.

I sniffed them and nearly fell over from the shock. I flopped down on them, then rubbed and wiggled my whole body. Parker the Barker called this "getting your wolf on." He once told me all dogs will roll around on smelly things like poop, carcasses, or even socks. Our ancestors, he said, did that to cover their own scent before they would hunt. Every dog is born with that same instinct.

No coyote on earth would want to eat me now. I smelled as if I were already dead! I was a genius, and I wished Parker the Barker could be here to see it.

Oh. Wait.

What if that coyote knew this trick? Or what if coyotes *liked* stinky smells?

I gulped air, trying to calm my racing heart.

I might as well have been a rare ribeye steak, double dipped in Cowboy Costner's favorite fatback-flavored, greasy gravy, flaunting my special stink back and forth in front of a four-finned floor fan that was blowing the appetizing aroma of soured socks in the craving canine's dangerous direction.

I stopped for a second, listening to all the crazy talk in my head.

That was a lengthy laundry list of letters.

I get wordy when I'm worried, wondering what's wrong.

Ugh! I was doing it again. I had to stop talking to myself.

A twig snapped right outside our tent. I held my breath for a second, then yelled, "Mr. James?"

No answer. I called out again and again, but Mr. James never replied.

Did he leave me? Will he come back? How am I going to get out of this tent? Where will I go?

Finally, I saw Mr. James's head rise slightly above the edge of the bank. He was using the tin coffee cup to scoop water from the stream and dump it on his head. I saw him do this a few times, and then he grabbed a towel and dried his hair.

He walked back to the tent, whistling. "Whew! That water was cold, but it sure felt refreshing."

He seemed happy until he looked at me. I knew he could see the fear in my eyes.

"Ruby, what's wrong?"

"I thought you weren't coming back," I said softly, embarrassed.

He wrinkled his nose. "What is that smell?"

"I was afraid that a coyote was going to eat me, so I used your socks as a self-defense weapon."

He rubbed his eyes as if they were stinging. "I guess I better wash those next."

I tried to smile, but a tear slipped down my cheek.

He reached out and lifted my chin so he could look right into my eyes. "Ruby, I understand why you were afraid. When you were just a few weeks old, someone abandoned you, leaving you in a shelter. It's natural to be afraid that someone will abandon you again. I promised you I will never abandon you, and I won't. You just have to trust me."

"How do I learn to trust, Mr. James?"

"Trust starts when you accept that no one is perfect and everyone makes mistakes. You can't trust people to be perfect, because no one is. You can trust that the right people will love you, even if they make mistakes, and even if you make mistakes too. Trust means you're not afraid to see where a road takes you."

I nodded thoughtfully. "Mr. James, I trust you."

"Good." Mr. James rolled up the tent, the sleeping bag, and my towel. He kicked dirt on top of the campfire until the fire was completely out, just like the Smokey the Bear signs said to do. Then he used the tip of his shoe to draw the words "Ruby and James were here" in the dirt.

"Now," he said, "we have to see where a new road can take us." Pulling his map from the backpack, he used his finger to draw a straight line on the map from where we were standing all the way down to Clovis, New Mexico.

"I can't walk on the interstate, and we can't keep walking on Route 66. The part ahead of us was removed when the Super Highway was built. So we have to find a new way."

We headed out, walking south.

A dog stood on top of a house and barked. He barked more than Parker the Barker did. Even I wanted to tell him to quiet down. We walked past a big airplane in a park and into Melrose, New Mexico.

Mr. James found a few more coins on the road and put them in his fanny pack.

"What are you going to do with all those coins you've found on the road?" I asked.

"I'm going to donate them to a charity when I get back home."

"Is it millions of dollars?"

"No. It's only a few dollars."

"A few dollars? How will that make a difference?"

"When I was a boy, I'd hunt for golf balls in the creeks and bushes on a golf course. When I found them, I'd sell them back to the golfers for twenty-five cents apiece. Sometimes I'd work all day and only earn two dollars. I'd save up my money until I had enough to buy a toy from the store. If that toy was twenty dollars, I had to have twenty dollars plus a little extra for taxes, or the clerk would not sell me the toy. So I learned that every penny counts."

"Or every quarter," I added.

"Right."

"Why didn't the clerk just give you the toy? Kids shouldn't have to work."

"Hard work is good for you, Ruby! Everyone should work and not expect to get anything free. Work keeps you focused and out of trouble. And there's nothing like the feeling you get when you earn your own money."

"I want to earn my own money and buy two postcards."

"Why two postcards?"

"I'd like to send them to Stella and Parker the Barker. But I'd have to find them first. I don't know who adopted them."

Mr. James grinned. "I know those names! You talk about them in your sleep."

I grinned too. I liked dreaming about friends. It made me feel like we were still together somehow.

❖

Here is a list of everything I saw between Clovis, New Mexico, and Fort Sumner, New Mexico:

- Three gas stations,
- Two spotted horses standing in a field swatting flies with their tails, and
- One train track that stretched for miles before disappearing into the horizon.

The only thing I couldn't count, because there was so much of it, was the sky. The sky was feathered blue, and at the far end, all the reddish-brown earth jumped up and met the sky for a kiss.

As we walked, the Santa Fe train chugged past us several times a day. The engineer pulled a cord hanging down over his head to blow the horn. He'd give us a thumbs-up and yell for his buddies to wave at "the country singer and his dog walking for foster kids."

I waved back. That made them laugh, as if a dog who could wave was very funny. They needed to get out more.

CHAPTER TWELVE

I was just beginning to doze off in the warm sun when Mr. James piped up. "Ruby! This is the village where Billy the Kid is buried." He sounded excited.

I poked my head out of the jacket. Mr. James was standing near a gravesite, reading a sign.

"His tombstone has been stolen three times," he said, "but fortunately, it's been returned all three times too."

"You can't blame that on me. I was at the shelter."

Mr. James laughed. "I'm not blaming you, Ruby. I'm trying to teach you about history. Don't you want to know why there is a steel cage around his tombstone?"

"Oh. Sorry. Yes."

He sighed. "Maybe I should have called you Ruby-the-Interrupting-Dog. Anyway—"

"Who's Billy the Kid?" I blurted.

"He was an Orphan Train kid. Later, he became a famous frontier criminal."

"What's an Orphan Train kid?"

"Well, now, that's a story. A long, long time ago, orphans and homeless kids wandered the streets of New York City. The police rounded them up, loaded them onto trains, and sent them out west. Whenever the train stopped at a depot, each of the kids got off the train and stood on a platform with a string and a numbered tag around his neck. Strangers would pinch the kids' arms to see how much

muscle they had. If a kid seemed healthy and strong enough to work, the stranger would call out the kid's number, sign a receipt, and then take the kid home. The kids were put to work mostly on farms. Many of the smaller kids were chosen last. Often, when the big kids were chosen, they had to leave their smaller brothers and sisters behind. The orphan train would chug away, and those siblings would never see each other again."

"They could text."

"No cell phones back then."

"Or send a postcard," I said.

"Most of them didn't get to go to school. I don't know how many could read or write."

"But you can't separate families!" I hollered. "That hurts worse than anything in the world!"

Mr. James reached up and gently petted my head. "You got separated from your family, didn't you?"

I nodded, too sad to speak. "Maybe that's why I was chosen last. Because I'm small. If I had been bigger, maybe my family could have stayed together."

"Ruby, when families get separated, it's never, ever the kid's fault." He looked down at me and grinned. His nostrils sure were big from this angle.

"I don't think your size had anything to do with when you were adopted. Stella was small, wasn't she? I think you just had to wait for the right person to come along. You needed someone to adopt you because they liked you."

Mr. James smiled! I smiled too. He liked me. That *was* worth waiting for. "What happened to the kids?"

"What kids?"

"The Orphan Train kids."

Mr. James took a deep breath. I could tell the story made him sad. "The Orphan Train was abolished in the late 1920s."

"Because they all got adopted and there were no more orphans?"

"There will always be orphans, Ruby. That's what I'm trying to tell the whole world. The Orphan Train didn't get abolished because they ran out of kids who needed homes, but because people got tired of seeing them."

I raised my ears. "What?"

"People who lived near the train stations complained to their leaders and politicians about all the 'vagabonds' being dropped off in their communities. That's when the US government created the foster care system. The kids have been struggling to be seen ever since that day."

I lowered my ears. I understood why he was sad.

"Now, Ruby, there are wonderful people who work within the foster care system. Every day they try to help the five hundred thousand foster children living in America. But they are overworked and underpaid. They get burnt out, and they don't make enough money to support their own families. These workers are just as important to children's safety and well-being as schoolteachers, police officers, fire fighters, linemen, and other emergency personnel."

"Do they wear uniforms, like policemen?"

"No. So you never know when you might be standing next to a real live hero."

I wagged my tail just a little. I was with a real live hero. But I was still worried about all those kids.

"Some people refuse to respect you until they need you. A worker who sacrifices so much to protect and serve others should always be treated well. Those people who ignore sacrifice and hard work are no better than outlaws."

"What's an outlaw?" I asked.

"An outlaw is someone who's broken the law but hasn't been captured by the police."

"Like Billy the Kid."

"Billy the Kid wasn't *always* an outlaw. He started life just like everyone else. He wanted a family and he wanted to be loved. But he didn't have either one. We only know his name today because he did bad things. We've forgotten the bad things that were done to him. People often point their fingers when they should be extending a helping hand."

"So what happened to Billy? Why did he become a criminal?"

"To survive, I suppose. He stole a pair of pants and then some food. Before long, he joined a gang. I think that gang became a family to him. People will always find a way to get what they need, Ruby."

"Mr. James, if you hadn't adopted me, I might have become an outlaw too."

He laughed. "Then we'd be outlaws together. I'd tuck you in a holster on my belt, and I'd warn all the bad guys: Don't make me use my Chihuahua!"

I did my best scary-mean face and growled, "Let me introduce you to my little friend."

Mr. James laughed so hard he had to wipe a tear from his eye. "Ruby, I'd take on any bad guy in the world with you at my side."

"But first we have to save those kids. And just so you know, I am part miniature pincher too."

Mr. James's eyes crinkled, then became sad. "If those kids are going to be saved, the church and the government have to help too."

I settled back down a bit and sighed. "What happened to Billy the Kid? Did someone eventually help him?"

"Billy the Kid was finally captured by his best friend, Pat Garrett, who was also a sheriff. Legend says Pat Garrett shot The Kid in the back."

"His best friend betrayed him?"

"Yep, he sure did."

"That's horrible. And then someone stole Billy's tombstone? Why would anyone steal a tombstone?"

"He became famous." Mr. James shrugged. "People love fame, even if someone is famous for the wrong reasons. People slapped Billy's name onto every piece of merchandise and real estate in the state of New Mexico. His name generated lots of money. Billy the Kid finally mattered to the public."

I stared at the horizon. "I hope, wherever he is now, that he's happy. I hope he sees that the whole state adopted him."

"Me, too, Ruby." He cleared his throat and sighed. "That's why there's a steel cage around the tombstone now.

So people don't steal it again."

I sighed as the memory of my own cage came back to me. Poor Billy the Kid. He never escaped his cage.

"It's okay, sweetheart." Mr. James stroked the fur between my shoulder blades. "The story has an interesting twist. The town turned the bad experiences into something good. They hold a Tombstone Race during the Old Fort Days festival every year here in Fort Sumner."

"What's a tombstone race?"

"Each contestant runs ten yards and jumps a four-foot hurdle. Then they run ten more yards and jump a five-foot hurdle. They pick up a tombstone that weighs ninety pounds, run back, and throw the tombstone back over the five-foot hurdle. They pick up the stone again, run, and toss it over the four-foot hurdle. They pick up the stone a third time, place it inside a square chalk box, and sprint back across the two hurdles to the finish line. The winner gets a prize."

"That sounds very hard to do."

"I bet it is. I try not to carry anything more than five pounds."

I grinned and nuzzled his chin, glad I didn't weigh six pounds.

He nuzzled me right back. "The Tombstone Race brings people together for the day."

On the way out of Fort Sumner, Mr. James stopped in at the Cortese Feed and Supply store and had a cup of black coffee. The folks there were very nice. Why couldn't everyone be nice?

"Have you ever been betrayed, Mr. James?"

"Betrayal is part of life. We have to decide whether to carry a grudge or forgive. I choose not to carry grudges.

They weigh too much, way more than a tombstone. Plus, Jesus is the only one who had the right to carry a grudge. Instead, He carried a cross."

"Is a cross as heavy as a tombstone?"

"It's a lot heavier. Imagine carrying the burden of everyone's sins. That means every bad deed, bad word, bad thought … all piled up onto one person's back. That's how much a cross weighs."

"I could never carry that."

"Me neither. That's why Jesus carried it for us."

CHAPTER THIRTEEN

Walking into Yeso, New Mexico, Mr. James discovered a package on the ground beside the road.

"Is it treats that someone dropped off for me?" I asked, watching as Mr. James examined the package.

The paper and string looked dry and bleached from the desert sun. He carefully removed the string, unfolded the paper, and discovered a stack of family photos inside. On top of the stack was an ultrasound photo with a date written at the bottom.

"That baby is at least nine years old now," he said.

"I wonder where that kid is today, Mr. James."

"There's no telling, Ruby. I don't know who the baby is. But that random photo reminds me of the foster kids who are abandoned every day in America."

"Why do you care so much about foster kids? I know you said we're supposed to use our talents to serve others, but why do you want to help foster kids? You don't know any of them, either."

Mr. James stopped walking. He took me out of his jacket and set me on the ground beside him. "Because I was a foster kid, too, Ruby."

My eyes widened with surprise. Mr. James had been a foster kid?

We began walking again, and I waited for him to tell me more.

Finally, Mr. James spoke. "I know exactly what it's like walking in their shoes. I know what it's like to be hungry and have nothing to eat. I know what it's like to be abandoned on the side of the road by your parents, and then stand at the bus stop waiting to be rescued. I know what it's like to be hopeless."

There was another long moment of silence. I wondered if Mr. James was going to cry.

"But Ruby, I also know what it's like to be rescued and given a loving home. I know what it's like to be given a comfortable bed to sleep in and a place to wash my clothes and take a shower. I know the feeling of unconditional love too. I had nothing to offer the family that opened their heart and home to me. I was sixteen years old and homeless. This family's kindness gave me the opportunity to complete high school, go to college, and then chase and even catch my dream. I wouldn't be who I am today if that foster family hadn't rescued me. That's why I'm walking for foster kids. I don't know them personally, but I know what it's like to *be* one."

"I'm glad you're helping those kids just like that family helped you. And I'm glad you adopted me."

"I am too, Ruby. We're supposed to give back. It's the right thing to do."

I nodded in agreement. But something nagged at me. We were supposed to give back, to do something, to help where we could. I began to wonder if I would ever have that chance.

We continued on Highway 285 into Vaughn, New Mexico. A car pulled over along the side the road up ahead of us. The driver rolled down his window and waved us over. A young lady sat in the passenger seat, smiling at us.

"You must be that guy who's walking for foster kids," the man said. "The DJ on the radio was just talking about you! I'd like to pay for a room tonight for you and your pup there if you don't mind. It's my way of showing my appreciation."

Mr. James accepted his offer. As we rode in the backseat, they told us they were on their way home to New York after visiting a college in California and had decided to take the scenic route through southern New Mexico. The daughter seemed more excited about the college in California than the father did.

We stopped by the front desk of Penny's Diner, where guests had to check in to get a key for a room at the Oak Tree Inn. After the nice man paid the lady, she gave Mr. James the key plus a to-go order of food.

That night Mr. James washed some clothes in the bathtub with hand soap. He made a clothes-drying line by tying a string between a chair and the doorknob.

It sure was nice sleeping in a comfortable bed again. I missed seeing the stars overhead, though.

Our adventure continued the next morning. We met wonderful people every day.

One lady paid for our lunch at the Willard Cantina & Cafe.

We met the Cain family in Mountainair, New Mexico, who allowed me and Mr. James to stay in their vacant trailer for the night. My heart felt light. Mr. James had seen a lot of sadness in his life, but people were good to him, and that made me happy.

Nine miles west of Mountainair was a national landmark called Abó. Abó is an ancient ruin from the fourteenth century. When we got there, Mr. James took off his shoes and rested. His socks fit right in with the ruins. Soap was never going to fix those things. They smelled like they hadn't been washed since the fourteenth century.

Here's a travel tip: When you're fifty miles outside of Socorro, New Mexico, between Magdalena and Datil, it looks like you're on the moon. There isn't anything to see but dust … and some weird cereal bowls.

Mr. James snapped pictures of the enormous white bowls that were mounted on railroad tracks. "They're amazing, aren't they?" he asked.

"I don't even know what they are," I said.

"You're looking at the VLA, which stands for Very Large Array. This is one of the world's biggest radio observatories. Those bowl-shaped things are satellites. There are twenty-seven of them, and together they can see UV energy and x-rays in outer space. They're out here on the plains because the terrain is flat and vast, so there's no interference."

"Why does anyone need to see UV energy and x-rays in outer space?"

"Well, there are many reasons, Ruby. One of those reasons is to study the weather. That's how news people know when a tornado is forming and can warn the authorities. The town can sound the tornado alarm so everyone can take cover. Just because we can't see something doesn't mean we can ignore it."

"So we use those cereal bowls to look into outer space?"

He nodded. "And the satellites up there look back down on us and take our picture."

"I would like to have my x-ray picture taken by one of those satellites."

"It's not just one individual satellite that takes a picture. All twenty-seven satellites join together, creating one big satellite that takes a picture."

"When they take a picture at night, do they have to turn on their flash?"

Mr. James just laughed. "I don't know. But maybe we can ask one of the astronomers if they'd be willing to snap a photo of you."

We walked down Service Road 166 off US 60 until we reached the control station, where a man wearing a hard hat was standing. He introduced himself as one of the controllers.

"Sir, my dog and I are walking to Phoenix, and we saw the VLA. Is there any chance that you can take an x-ray photo of Ruby?"

"Wh-what?" the man stuttered. "No one has their photo taken by the VLA. Those satellites take pictures of important things. Things like the Milky Way, black holes, and young stars in the solar system."

"Sir, my dog *is* important." Mr. James looked at the astronomer, and the astronomer looked at Mr. James. He then looked at me, then back at Mr. James, then back at me. I think the guy knew he was beat.

"Okay," he said with a sigh. "I'll take an x-ray photo of

Ruby. But she'll have to stand way out there in the open plains. All the satellites will turn toward her and snap the photo."

The three of us got into a vehicle that looked like an ice cream truck with a flashing orange emergency light on top. The astronomer drove out into the middle of the vast plain. He radioed a scientist back at the base with his walkie-talkie and told him to go ahead and snap the photo.

By the time we got back to the VLA, the x-ray was already printed. A scientist handed the photo to the astronomer and the astronomer held it up to the sunlight. He glanced at me, then back at the photo.

I fidgeted, getting nervous. What did he see?

"It looks like there's a whole lot of love in that little heart of yours."

I couldn't help but smile. The astronomer handed the x-ray photo to Mr. James.

"Thank you very much," Mr. James said.

"You're very welcome," replied the astronomer. "You know, I've seen a lot of stars in my career, but I've never seen one shine brighter than your little dog." He winked at me. "She had me at the underbite."

I must have blushed, because my cheeks got hot. It's a little embarrassing to be this good-looking.

Mr. James and I walked back down the service road and onto US 60 and then continued walking west.

CHAPTER FOURTEEN

Mr. James handed me a travel guide to read so I wouldn't get bored. I liked to read aloud to him. When we got close to our next stop, I read him what the book said about it.

"In the middle of nowhere, somewhere off US Highway 60, eight thousand feet above sea level, is a famous, rustic, frontier town that hardly anyone knows exists. It's called Pie Town. It was one of the most photographed areas in America because it illustrates the effects of the Great Depression. Its famous gelatin-silver photographs from the Great Depression are preserved in the archives of the Library of Congress in Washington DC, where all kinds of other cool photos and artifacts are kept."

I wondered what a gelatin-silver photograph might be. A photo made with fancy Jell-O, maybe?

"By the looks of these faded white lines on this scorched strip of asphalt," Mr. James said, "this road used to run through this town. Now it barely even walks."

I lowered the guidebook to stare at the road.

"I didn't know roads could run or walk, Mr. James. If they can, then why are *we* doing all the walking?"

Mr. James laughed. "It's just a figure of speech. This old road sure has seen many days in the hot sun, hasn't it? It just lies there like a cooked hot dog in a warm bun between those old, rundown houses. Speaking of hot dogs, I sure am hungry. I wish I could eat a New York City hot dog right here, right now."

I dropped the guidebook, startled. He was a dog-eater? I knew this adoption was not going to work! "What is a hot dog?" I yelled. "Is it a dog that got hot from walking miles in the summer heat, like we're doing, and got put into a bun?" I swallowed hard, fear rising up as I imagined my fate.

Mr. James shook his head. "A hot dog is a kind of food you can buy from the vendors in front of the Hearst building."

Maybe that was why Parker the Barker chose a pretzel instead of a hot dog when he was in New York. He was trying to warn me!

"Please don't give me to a vendor! I wouldn't want to get stuck in a bun and sold to somebody on the sidewalk in New York City."

Mr. James picked up the guidebook and laughed. "Ruby, that is ridiculous—and gross. A hot dog is a weenie. You add chili, mustard, and onions on top of it, and it's delicious."

"Why is it called a hot dog?"

"Because it was inspired by a dachshund. You know, the dogs with short legs and long bodies?"

Like Willie? I thought I was going to pass out. Why would anyone want to eat Willie?

Mr. James started whistling as he walked, as if he didn't have a care in the world. Must be nice, knowing you weren't going to end up in a bun.

Then I remembered something from long ago. A shelter worker had a hot dog for lunch one day ... and his breath smelled like sausage! It didn't smell like a dog at all.

"What is a hot dog made from, Mr. James?"

"Beef or pork, sometimes a mix of both," Mr. James said.

Whew! I breathed a sigh of relief. But then I got mad. Why did people always pick on dogs? "So why isn't it called a hot cat?"

"Ruby! This conversation is making my stomach queasy."

"Well, how do you think I feel?" I asked. "Has anyone ever said they wanted to throw you in a bun and squirt mustard on you and sell you on the street?"

"You're right, Ruby. A hot dog is a terrible name for this type of food, and I can see how that made you feel bad." He paused. "Gosh, I can't imagine if someone named a type of food a po' boy or shepherd's pie."

He'd ordered both of those dishes in diners. "Mr. James, you're being a smart aleck, aren't you?"

He laughed. "I'm sorry, Ruby. I guess all this walking and being isolated from the real world has made me a little delirious, but that's no excuse. Names are very important. And calling something, or someone, by the wrong name can be very hurtful. Even dangerous."

"Imagine not having a name at all," I grumbled. "Before you came along, I was just called a number."

"Imagine how the slaves from long ago felt, forced to accept their owners' names," Mr. James added. "Or a Jewish girl or boy forced to accept a new name from the Nazis."

"That's so sad! I'm thankful for my name. I like being Ruby."

"I'm thankful you allowed me to call you Ruby."

"I'm thankful you're thankful that I'm thankful."

"Ruby, don't start."

"Okay."

CHAPTER FIFTEEN

A few yards ahead, I saw a sign standing in the grass beside the road. The sign had a picture of three pies, and the yellow words above proclaimed this to be "Pie Town."

"Let's hope there's a good reason they call this town 'Pie Town,'" Mr. James said.

As we walked the dusty road into town, twelve rusted and weathered windmills stood still, silently guarding the lonely remains of what looked like a forgotten town.

I sniffed the air hopefully. No hints of pie.

Ahead, a lonely blue-and-white phone booth leaned to one side, pushed around by the winds and time. Weeds stretched up all around it. Mr. James put his hand to his ear. "Do I hear a pie calling my name?" he said.

I groaned. He thought *my* jokes were bad.

We walked along a rusty wire fence, and Mr. James tapped the battered vintage Coca-Cola sign wired to it, making everything sway. The fence surrounded a yard with an antique children's wagon abandoned in it. Colorful glass bottles in all shapes and sizes hung from the limbs of an old oak tree. Some bottles hung high and some hung low, just like those colorful balloons at the Albuquerque International Balloon Fiesta advertised on the billboard a few miles back. But still no pies. I didn't even see any people.

A yellow, blue, and red metal sign shaped like a Thunderbird perched high above a gravel parking lot near the Pie-O-Neer Café. The sign commanded us to "STOP."

"This must be where the pies are," Mr. James said.

A sweet aroma wafted through the air, making my nose twitch.

"Do you smell that, Ruby?" he asked as he lifted his nose high in the air too.

"I sure do, Mr. James."

"It's pie!" we both said at the same time.

"I think it's cherry," Mr. James added.

"And I smell apple!" I yelled.

We followed the delicious smell across the gravel parking lot to the steps of the Pie-O-Neer Café. The building was made of light yellow bricks with a sunbaked, barn-wood facade. I felt like we were in the Old West.

The wooden trim around each window was painted turquoise, and there were flowerpots on the edge of the front porch. The sunflowers in each one were lilting, heavy from the afternoon heat.

A new screen door hung in a very old doorframe, making me wonder what the original door had looked like. On the open-air porch, an old wooden church pew sat beside a tall wooden brown bear that had been carved with a chainsaw. Six columns held up a roof that looked like it belonged on a shed. A wooden sign shaped like a pie hung from a metal holder nailed to one of columns.

Mr. James picked me up and put me inside his jacket, then walked up the steps and onto the porch. He studied the welcome sign for a minute and then pulled open the screen door. The spring squeaked loudly.

A black oil-drum stove sat in the middle of the café on

the wooden floor. A long burnt pipe connected to the top of it stretched all the way up through the ceiling. Black-and-white photos and colorful paintings were tacked to the walls. News clippings were taped to the cash register. Gypsy beads draped over a doorway to the right that led to a room where used items were for sale. Red-chili lights were strung around the edge of the doorway leading to the kitchen. Square metal chairs and round wooden tables were arranged throughout the dining area. Nothing seemed to match, but everything fit together perfectly. Kind of like me and Mr. James.

A brown-haired woman wearing a white toque sat at one of the tables, peeling peaches with a knife and dumping the slices into a big, white bowl. She was the very first Pie-O-Neer person I'd ever laid eyes on.

She never took her eyes off the knife as she worked, but she smiled. "Have a seat anywhere you like. I'm Kathy, the owner of the Pie-O-Neer Café. I'd greet you proper, but I'm working on another pie."

I sniffed the air. She was working on a peach pie, but somewhere there was a chocolate pie cooling. When I sniffed again, I was sure there was a blueberry pie too.

Mr. James walked to the far left corner of the café and sat down on a green stool at the counter under a Red Baron toy airplane hanging from the ceiling. He took me out of his jacket and set me on the stool beside him.

"This stool reminds me of the ones we sit on when we're onstage," Mr. James said.

A young girl wearing a yellow-and-white pinstriped apron carried a stainless-steel coffeepot to us, a mug hooked around her thumb. She set the mug down and poured coffee for Mr. James. Returning a moment later, she poured fresh water from a clear pitcher into a ceramic bowl for me.

"Can I take your orders?" she asked politely. I smiled at her. She seemed nice.

"Yes, ma'am. I'll take some of that cherry pie. I could smell it baking from all the way up the road. And one of those healthy doggie pie biscuits in that jar, please."

"Coming right up!" She turned on her heel and disappeared into the kitchen.

"When did you start eating healthy doggie pie biscuits, Mr. James?"

Mr. James just looked out of the corner of his eye and said, "That healthy doggie pie biscuit is for you."

"It is?"

The young lady returned with a saucer that had a piece of cherry pie on it. She set it on the tile countertop. The piecrust was made of hearts. Another saucer held a healthy doggie pie biscuit. I sniffed it hopefully.

Mr. James held my paw and closed his eyes while praying over our meal. Although I wanted pie, I still thanked God for the biscuit. I'm sure those innocent dogs at the shelter would've given anything for this chance.

Mr. James smacked his chops between big bites, complimenting the baker. "This pie is the best I've ever had."

He noticed I hadn't eaten a bite of the biscuit. "Hey, I know you must be hungry, but slow down," he teased.

I didn't smile. I just stared at the floor. "Who wants a dog biscuit when there's hot, fresh pies coming out of the oven?"

"Oh, Ruby, I'm so sorry. That was very selfish of me not to include you in the pie tasting."

Mr. James waved to the girl and asked if he could get "a small sliver of pie for my little dog."

"Of course! I'll be right back."

The lady returned with the piece of cherry pie and set it down in front of me. I took my sweet time, enjoying every single crumb. After I finished, I licked my jowls and paws and even licked the plate.

While I ate, the girl asked Mr. James, "What brings you and your sweet pup to Pie Town?"

As he explained what he was doing and why, the girl stood with her hands in her back jean pockets and slightly rocked back and forth on her heels and toes while nodding her head.

She said she was from New York and had moved to Pie Town ten years ago.

"What made you move away from the Big Apple to little Pie Town?" Mr. James asked.

"The concrete wears your soles down. Besides, I needed to get away from all the hustle and bustle and find a little peace of mind."

"I understand," Mr. James said.

They talked some more. I was beginning to wonder if I should order more pie.

More customers arrived, and soon laughter filled the café, and more fresh pies came out of the oven. Some folks were visiting from other states and countries, and others were locals.

A man dressed in a silver suit removed his silver motorcycle helmet from his silver-haired head and sat down on the stool beside me. I glanced behind me out the front window. His motorcycle was silver too. He caught me peeking at it and smiled.

"I've wanted to ride a motorcycle on Highway 60 since I was a teenager," he said. "I read an article in a 1956 issue of *Arizona Highways* magazine and fell in love with it."

His accent was very different from anyone else's. I cocked my head, listening, and he laughed.

"I'm from Australia."

Another man sat by Mr. James. He had a thick black mustache that looked like a caterpillar sleeping under his nose. When Mr. James introduced himself, the stranger said he was a rock 'n' roll guy from Pittsburgh. Before Mr. James could reply, the guy said, "It's a shame what Route 66 did to Highway 60."

CHAPTER SIXTEEN

A man who looked like a gentle old grandfather took a seat nearby. The waitress pointed him out to me. "He's one of the original Pie Town homesteaders. The locals call him Pops. He's the best farmer in the community."

Pops blushed a bit and nodded to me. I raised my paw and waved.

When he cleared his throat to speak, a hush fell over the café. "I remember when they put Route 66 in," he said. The sound of his voice was deep and strong, a voice that demanded attention and respect.

"It diverted all the traffic northeast, away from Highway 60. In those years, trucks had taken the place of trains. Farmers had a hard time shipping their crops, like grain and vegetables. In small places like Pie Town, no one could make a living anymore. Many of my friends loaded up everything they owned and moved closer to Route 66 and the truckers. A drought hit the land and nearly wiped all of us out. Then, just when we were scrambling to recover, a terrible thing happened."

Everyone held their breath. I leaned in.

"The land turned on us. Some of the newer farmers hadn't understood what she needed or how to work her. When the wind blew hard, the land became a dust storm, the likes of which I pray I never see again."

He paused to wipe his eyes, like there was still dust in them all these years later. "Our land became known as the Dust Bowl. Summer winds kicked dust ten thousand feet in the air and carried it as far as New York City. The Dust Bowl destroyed just about everything in its path. Those who survived moved west toward California, looking for jobs. Some of those folks came back to Pie Town and settled down. I was just a little boy when my dad drove a John Deere tractor from Texas to a piece of land across the road. I've been here ever since."

"See there, Ruby?" Mr. James whispered. "Everyone goes through storms."

I gulped. I had never heard of a storm made of dust.

A man with a long, white beard who was sitting at the counter broke the silence. "The pies were just as delicious back then as they are now," he said.

Everyone laughed.

He introduced himself to us as Tony Shannon. He and his wife, Joan, drove their Winnebago east from California to Pie Town. They took a left turn off Highway 60, then drove three miles out across the plains before deciding to settle here.

"You didn't have a plan or know where you were going?" Mr. James asked. "You just drove until you reached Pie Town and decided to stop here?"

"Yes! It was that simple. Joan and I fell in love with the town the second we arrived. We decided there was no other place on earth we would rather be," Tony said.

Joan picked me up and petted me on my head. While the men talked, she walked me around the café and showed me all the photos and posters.

Then a woman burst through the screen door, a great big smile on her face. Some of the customers hollered a welcome to her, and Joan hugged her neck.

"Say hi to Nita," Joan told me.

"Hello, Nita. I'm Ruby. And see that scruffy guy over there? I live in his jacket."

She glanced at Mr. James, who waved hello.

"Are you a local?" I asked.

"Nope," she replied, moving to the counter to place her order. "I moved to Pie Town from Hawaii."

"Wow!" Mr. James raised his eyebrows. "The pies are good here, but I'm not sure I'd move from Hawaii just for that."

"Well, now, I didn't come here looking for pie. But once I got here, I realized the people were worth staying for. It's a very long story, but let's just say I would never trade Pie Town for a palm tree."

When Nita heard about the walk Mr. James and I were on, she offered us a spare room for the night at the Toaster House.

"What's a Toaster House?" I asked.

"It's a hostel, a home where travelers can stay if they don't have enough money for a hotel room," Nita said. "And around here, there aren't really any hotels anyway."

"I appreciate the offer," Mr. James said.

"There's only one rule. You can have any food in the freezer you want, but please leave a few dollars in its place. That way I can purchase more food, and other travelers can have something to eat when they stay at the Toaster House."

"That's very generous of you," Mr. James said.

Mr. James took the last bite of his second slice of cherry pie and sipped the last few drops of coffee in his cup. He left a generous tip in the jar by the cash register.

"Thank you very much!" Our waitress seemed very glad to get a tip. I had one for her too: stop selling dog biscuits. Dogs prefer pie.

Joan handed me to Mr. James, and he put me inside his jacket.

The owner was pulling pies out of the oven and setting them on a windowsill. The window was open, and the red tablecloth curtains danced softly in the wind above the hot pies. Mr. James waved to her.

"See ya again real soon!" The café family had already adopted us, I think. That was a good feeling.

Back on the dusty road, Mr. James said, "Ruby, this town is unlike any place I've ever been. The people are different from anyone else I've ever met. It's like being in a completely different world."

"Maybe they're not really people. Maybe they're Martians who flew their UFOs down here."

"Martians, huh? That would explain why they're so nice. But how do you know what a UFO is?" he asked.

"Didn't you see the poster on the wall in the café? It was a pie coming down from the sky and landing on the earth. One of the Martians getting out of it looked just like the rock 'n' roll man with the caterpillar mustache."

"Maybe that's why he likes to rock it. Get it? *Rocket.*" He slapped his knee and laughed so hard he wheezed. He really loved his own jokes, especially after having dessert.

I frowned at him. "Don't start, Mr. James."

We continued on Highway 60, but within minutes, a dark cloud moved in from the south. Rain began falling hard. Lightning flashed in the open plain. My stomach twisted into a knot.

"A tornado's coming!" I yelled, ducking deeper into the jacket.

Mr. James decided to take Nita up on her offer and stay the night at the Toaster House.

CHAPTER SEVENTEEN

Toasters hung by their cords from the trees and fence that surrounded the house.

"This must be it," Mr. James said. "The famous Toaster House."

Thunder rumbled closely, and lightning popped again.

"We need to get inside immediately," Mr. James said, running up onto the porch of the Toaster House. I was bouncing around inside his jacket.

We got out of the storm just in time. Ice started pounding the ground, followed by more thunder and lightning. It was a hailstorm, and a bad one.

"Whew! Thank God for people like Nita," Mr. James said, "or we'd be stuck in that storm. Lightning and trekking poles is a very bad combination."

I swallowed nervously. I was glad I hadn't known that before.

Looking around, the first thing I noticed on the porch was a bunch of shoes hanging by their shoestrings from nails in the wall. A sign read, "Take a pair if you need one, or leave a pair for someone else." By the door, another note said, "Come on in! The door is unlocked."

Mr. James carefully opened the door and walked inside.

A big sign-in book sat on the kitchen table. People from all over the world who'd stayed at the Toaster House had scrawled their names. Turning to a blank page, Mr. James signed our names.

I kept looking around. There was so much to see! Whatnots and trinkets were placed in every nook and cranny. A bookshelf was stocked with cassette tapes. An old cooking stove sat next to that, and on top, a red plastic skull with black eyes watched me. I shook off the shivers and noticed colorful rocks perched everywhere, and a long rattlesnake skin draped over an old photo and some old bottles. I glanced under the table, hoping that snake wasn't going to come back looking for his skin.

The hail and rain continued beating the tin roof of the Toaster House. Mr. James found a spot to set his backpack down and unroll his sleeping bag. I sat on the sleeping bag, grateful for a soft spot to rest while the storm raged. Mr. James sat next to me, and I cuddled close for comfort.

While we waited for the storm to pass, two more guys hurried inside the Toaster House, shaking rain off their jackets. When they saw us, they introduced themselves.

"Hullo, I'm Luke."

"And I'm Adam. We are peddling across America on bicycles to raise awareness for troops back home in England."

Mr. James stood and shook their hands. "It's nice meeting you. My name is James and this is my dog, Ruby."

While they unpacked, Mr. James found an old brown guitar leaning against the wall in the corner.

To pass the time, Mr. James played a few songs, the guys shared a few stories, and then Tony and Joan from the Pie-O-Neer Café stopped by.

"We were hoping you'd be here," Tony said. "We just wanted to make sure you and Ruby were safe."

A few minutes later, a few more people from the Pie-O-Neer Café stopped by. Before long, there were about fifteen people in the Toaster House. Kathy even brought some pies. I was full of pie, but I couldn't resist.

"This must be where hikers and bikers find shelter when there's a storm," Mr. James said.

"We all need a safe place we can run to when there's a storm," Tony replied.

I nodded. Storms weren't so bad if you had a safe place to stay.

Everyone was laughing, playing instruments, and singing. It was the best party I'd ever been to.

Actually, it was the first and only party I'd ever been to. I decided I liked parties very much.

"Nita," Mr. James asked, "what inspired you to offer up a home like this to thousands of complete strangers?"

"I was in the yard one day and saw a few hikers. The Continental Divide passes in front of the house, you know. I offered them some watermelon and told them they were welcome to stay the night if they wanted to. The front door hasn't been locked since."

Mr. James shook his head in admiration and then called it a night. He cleaned our spot and climbed a ladder that led to a loft. He crawled inside the Marmot sleeping bag and zippered it halfway. Then he spread my light-blue towel on the inside flap of the sleeping bag. I curled up and lay down beside him. Our noses were almost touching. We could still hear music and laughter from downstairs.

"Ruby, I love small towns like this. There's equity, community, loyalty, and love. This town also reminds me of foster kids and dogs, like you."

"How so?"

"When Pops was sharing a piece of the Pie Town story earlier today at the Pie-O-Neer, it reminded me how America has turned its back on foster children. If Highway 60 mattered, Pie Town would not be struggling every day. If foster children mattered, they wouldn't be struggling every day. If dogs mattered, they wouldn't be struggling in shelters. It seems like highways, foster kids, and stray dogs only matter when we want them to. Unless you're Route 66, Superman, or Rin Tin Tin, you don't matter. You know, Superman was a foster kid too." He chuckled. "You probably have no idea who I'm talking about."

"I know Rin Tin Tin was a movie star," I said. "I heard about him in the shelter. He was a big deal."

"He sure was. Rin Tin Tin was a male German shepherd rescued by an American soldier from a World War I battlefield in France. He ended up in a movie that became a box-office hit. After that, he appeared in twenty-seven Hollywood films! Rin Tin Tin's success even rescued the movie company from bankruptcy. People all over the world loved Rin Tin Tin because he was a hero."

"But any dog can be a hero," I said. "Even a foster dog. You just have to give us a chance."

"Exactly!" Mr. James sounded excited. "We need to give everyone, especially these foster kids, a chance."

"Are you glad you gave me a chance, Mr. James?" I whispered, too embarrassed to say it very loud.

"Oh, Ruby, before I met you, all I did on the road was walk and think. I've probably thought about everything that ever happened to me at least four or five times. I called it 'priming the well.' I needed to cleanse my mind and heart from all the years that had made me calloused and hardened my heart. My heart was as hard as those asphalt roads when I started. I didn't let anyone or anything in. Now, having a clear mind and a soft heart has made me vulnerable. Even a mere bird flying in the sky, its wings flapping freely, can bring tears to my eyes. And you, my sweet little four-legged friend, have brought me so much joy over these past few weeks."

"What could possibly make someone like you become calloused and hard like the road we've been walking on?"

He sighed. "Ruby, it's amazing how the music business, or any business for that matter, can affect you, especially when you're making lots of money and busy being 'famous.' It can have a negative impact on you before you even realize it. Before you know it, you're caught up in it, you're desensitized, and your mind and heart become cluttered with all kinds of junk that shouldn't be there. This can happen to anyone trying to be successful, not just country singers. There's an old saying: with every new level there's a new devil. That means greed, pride, or … well, you get my point. This walk has really given me a lot of time to 'prime the well' and get a fresh perspective. You came into my life at the perfect time. Not only did I adopt you, Ruby … you adopted me. You helped me just as much as I helped you, probably even more. Ruby, remember when I said, 'Love is when you care so much for another person's heart that you want to be completely unselfish'? Well, I love you, little pal."

"If I'd been adopted by another family, I could have had a big yard just like Parker the Barker talked about. But there's no other place I would rather be right now, and there's no one I'd rather be with than you, Mr. James. Although you don't look like a normal foster parent, you are the perfect foster parent for me. We fit together like a pair of shoes walking on asphalt."

Just like Pie Town faded away before the Dust Bowl, the music faded into the background, and we fell asleep.

CHAPTER EIGHTEEN

"We have just under three miles before we reach the Arizona state line. That means less talking and more walking," Mr. James said. He huffed and puffed, anxious to get there before the sun went down.

"Well, then, save your breath and move those legs!" I barked.

"Two miles left!" I cheered a bit later.

"One mile left!" I yelled as we got closer.

He handed me the camera, and I snapped a photo of the one-mile sign.

When we had just fifty yards to go, I hollered, "Keep walking!" Mr. James paused and spoke to an invisible audience. "For all the foster children out there—I walked for you."

Suddenly a news van pulled over on the side of the road in front of us, and a redheaded woman jumped out, carrying a microphone. A guy with a big camera on his shoulder jumped out next. He pointed the camera in our direction.

"Coming to you live

just outside of Springerville." The redheaded woman had lots of makeup on, as if this was a special occasion. I licked my paw and tried my best to smooth down Mr. James's scruffy beard.

"What's going on?" he asked.

She stuck the microphone in his face. "Sir, we'd like you to tell us about your dog."

What? They weren't here to interview Mr. James?

"She's the only dog in history to ever have an x-ray photo taken by the VLA."

Mr. James pointed a finger at me. "She sure is!"

"What kind of dog is she?" she asked. "And why are you walking across America with her?"

"Why don't you ask her that? She's the one you should be interviewing."

The reporter raised an eyebrow, then held the microphone near my nose. The camera operator turned the camera downward.

Did Mr. James really want me to speak to another human being? On national—or at least local—television? I was so nervous my whole body shook. I ducked my head back into the backpack, but Mr. James reached in and grabbed me. He set me on the ground then backed up, resting against a post.

Overhead, a sign with a star and sunrays said, "The Grand Canyon State Welcomes You." I sure didn't feel welcomed. I felt terrified.

I looked at him, then looked back at the camera, then looked at him again.

"Go on. Tell her."

I hoped I didn't have anything in my teeth.

"Um … My name is Ruby."

The reporter and the cameraman gasped.

"I am a Chihuahua and miniature pinscher mix. Mr. James adopted me from an animal shelter. That's him over there."

I looked at Mr. James again, the same way kids look at their parents when they're nervous.

He smiled back at me. "Keep going, Ruby. You're doing great," he said.

"Mr. James is walking halfway across America to raise awareness for foster children who are aging out of foster care. Since they don't have families, a lot of them end up homeless."

The reporter frowned, as if she thought I was making that up. Or maybe she thought Mr. James was a ventriloquist.

"It's true! Every day, good kids end up on the streets, with no one to help them or keep them safe. Mr. James wants to help by letting everyone know about that. I'm just riding along to keep him company."

"He sounds pretty special." The reporter smiled. "And you are too. People all over the world have seen your photo at the VLA. Your picture is on T-shirts, hats, even smart phone cases. You're in every newspaper and magazine. Tell our viewers the story behind the photo taken at the VLA."

I shared the story, turning my head back and forth because I didn't know which side was my good one.

"Is there anything else you'd like to say to everyone out there watching? Maybe something about what Mr. James is really like when he's not on stage singing? Is he going to put you in one of his music videos?" The reporter smiled at me, then turned to smile at the camera. Her teeth were so white they twinkled.

I looked at Mr. James again. He nodded, a serious look on his face. The reporter had ignored everything I had said! All she wanted to talk about was a famous dog.

"Yes!" I said, moving closer to the microphone. "There is something I would like to say to everyone watching."

She giggled nervously, using a hand to smooth her hair for the camera as she faced me.

"Innocent dogs are waiting in shelters to be adopted by someone who cares. Go to your local shelter and adopt a dog now. They need your help just like kids need your help. Please, don't let time run out on any of us!"

She rolled her eyes, but the camera didn't catch it. Then she walked away, not even turning around to say thank you. "We got what we need."

The news crew loaded up the camera equipment and raced away.

Mr. James looked at me, smiling big. "I'm so proud of you, Ruby. You handled that interview like a real star. You shined for others."

I shrugged. If that reporter didn't care about foster kids or dogs, why would anyone else be interested?

The following morning people came and walked with us to show their support. People showed up everywhere I looked! I didn't realize how many people would see the interview.

The Dairy Queen in Show Low served Mr. James and me each a Starkiss ice cream bar. The checkout lady at the IGA grocery store in Herber waved her hand through the window as we walked by. Above the store, an American flag waved in the wind.

"The stars and stripes are so beautiful, aren't they?" Mr. James said.

I nodded. This country was filled with beauty, and the people were the best part.

As we walked, Mr. James's phone kept ringing. Every time he hung up, he had something new to tell me.

"That was someone from a magazine."

"That was someone from a movie company."

"That was another newspaper."

His tone changed completely after the next call.

"That was an ex-girlfriend."

"What is an ex-girlfriend?" I asked.

"An ex-girlfriend is someone who *used* to be a girlfriend. She called because she saw your interview on the local news station back in Nashville."

"Why isn't she still your girlfriend?"

"Well, whenever I told her I loved her, she'd always say I love U2."

"If she said she loved you too, why is she an ex-girlfriend?"

"Ruby, I'm friends with a U2 cover band. They play U2 songs, but they aren't the real group. She loved the guys in the cover band, and she liked that I could get her free front-row tickets to their shows. After a while, she decided she liked the guy who sold their merchandise at shows. He could get her free front-row seats *and* free T-shirts. She didn't want me anymore." He sighed. "In life, some people don't want you; they just want what you can do for them."

I growled.

"Exactly how I feel," he said. "Later, I became friends with the real U2 rock band. She sure missed out, in more ways than one."

"Too bad for her!" I agreed.

"Her timing has always been impeccable." Mr. James sounded mad, the kind of mad that sticks around and puts down deep roots.

I cleared my throat, a little nervous about what I had in mind to say. I could tell Mr. James any of my secrets, but telling him the truth? That was scary.

"Maybe God's timing is impeccable," I said quietly. "You have to forgive her now and let it go."

He shrugged and kept walking.

I tapped him on the chest with my paw, emphasizing my point. "You should let go of the things you can't control. What she did was wrong, but it's also wrong to stay mad. Besides, saying good-bye to her left space available in your jacket for me."

"Ruby, I never carried her around in my jacket."

"You made her walk everywhere?"

Mr. James seemed exasperated with me, so I had to talk

fast. "Remember what you said about carrying a grudge? It sounds like you need to repent, ask forgiveness, and move on."

"A real friend tells it like it is," he said quietly. "You're right, again, Ruby."

"Every time." I grinned to myself and hoped he couldn't tell how fast my heart was beating.

We trudged several thousand feet down the White Mountains, through Star Valley into Payson. The view around us changed from lush pine trees to prickly cactuses.

"This is like Baldwin Street!" Mr. James said. "That's the steepest street in the world. The houses have to be built with stilts on one side."

"Stilts?" I was confused.

"The stilts level the house. Without them, you'd get out of bed and slide all the way to the other end of the house. Talk about rolling out of bed in the morning!"

I shook my head. He loved puns.

"Baldwin Street is in New Zealand," he said. "When we get home, I'll look it up on the Internet and show you."

"That sounds pretty far," I murmured.

"Sure hurts my foot to walk at this steep angle," Mr. James said.

I didn't really pay attention. Looking around, I was nervous. We were the only living things out on the road.

Or so we thought. Suddenly I heard strange scraping, rattling noises in the distance. The hairs on my back lifted. Something didn't feel right.

"There are so many stars in the sky tonight; it looks like there are a million holes in the floor of heaven," Mr. James said. He was looking up.

He should have been looking down.

A state trooper pulled over his patrol car. "I'm Officer Lamb," he said as he rolled down his window. "You need to be extra careful out here. This is the Beeline Highway, the deadliest state route in Arizona."

My heart pounded in my chest. I could feel Mr. James's heart speed up too.

The officer motioned for us to stand out of the way and then he hit his lights on their brightest setting. Mr. James and I searched the road ahead, but all we saw were a bunch of rocks in the pavement.

Then one of them uncoiled its long, scaly body and slithered into the shrubs on the other side.

Rattlesnakes filled the road ahead as far as I could see! Everywhere I looked, rattlesnakes lay coiled, their tongues flicking out, tasting the air. Tasting *me*!

"Why don't their eyes reflect the light?" Mr. James asked. "I thought if I had a flashlight I'd be safe out here."

"Their eyes aren't like ours. They rely on the heat-sensing pits on their heads, and those don't reflect light. If you're not careful, you can walk right up to one at night and not even know it … until it's too late."

They could swallow me in one bite. I gulped.

"Walk on ahead of me," Officer Lamb said, "and I'll shine my spotlight on the road ahead for you. You need a big, bright light to get through this territory."

True to his word, he followed behind us with his spotlight shining on the road.

Angry snakes shook their rattles when we got too close, but they stayed away from us. Mr. James concentrated on walking along the dangerous road, staying in the center of the light.

"Ruby, remember when I said a star shines the way so others can see? That's exactly what Officer Lamb is doing for us."

"We'd be dead if he hadn't come along," I whispered.

He chuckled. "I like his name too. The Lamb is leading the blind tonight. That's for sure."

Then he reached up and petted my shaky body. "We're safe, Ruby, because we're walking in the light. This is just like our walk with God. We have to pay attention and focus on every step we take. Sometimes evil will warn you when you get too close; other times, it won't. We may have to walk a little slower, or go a little farther to avoid danger. It may wear your shoes down, but it'll save your soul."

A rattle warned us to move carefully. Mr. James got quiet, concentrating on getting us out of there alive. I never thought I would say this, but that night, a Lamb saved my life.

Early the next morning, Mr. James's cell phone rang. By his voice, I could tell it wasn't anyone he knew.

"She's right here beside me," he said.

"We should be there August first," he said a minute later. Suddenly he got a big grin on his face. "OK, then, we'll see y'all there!" He hung up and rubbed my ears, deep in thought, then ran his hands through his hair. Something big was up.

"Ruby, that was a lady who said she saw you on her local news station in White Deer, Texas. She is going to meet us at the finale."

"Mr. James has a new girlfriend, na-na-na-na-na-na," I teased in a sing-song voice.

"Ruby …"

I could tell from the seriousness in his eyes that Mr. James needed to tell me something important. So I stopped playing around.

"You remember Stella from the shelter, right?"

My heart leaped. "Of course." How could I forget that sweet Chihuahua who gave birth to litters of puppies every year until she got too old and the breeder didn't want her anymore. "Is she okay?"

Mr. James nodded to the phone. "That was the woman who adopted Stella. Her name is Mercy. Stella asked her to help locate her pups, the ones that were taken from her right before she was dumped at the shelter. Mercy tracked down the puppy mill owner. He wasn't too happy about being caught dumping Stella like that but—"

"But what about Stella?" I interrupted.

He held up a hand to tell me to be patient … and quiet.

"The puppy mill owner gave her the number of the family that purchased one of Stella's pups. Mercy contacted the family, but they didn't have the puppy anymore. Turns out, they dropped the pup off at the shelter after having her for just two weeks."

"Well, that's rude," I blurted.

"Ruby, that pup was *you*."

"Wait! You mean someone adopted me when I was teeny-tiny, then they dumped me at the shelter? Why would they do that? What did I do?"

"Nothing, Ruby. Their son got very sick, and they just couldn't afford to take care of you because of the medical bills." He studied my face. "Ruby, do you know what this means?"

I wasn't sure what he was getting at. Then it hit me. "Stella's my mom?" I gasped. "Stella's my mom!" I yelled, my tail wagging so hard I thought it might leave bruises on my rump.

CHAPTER NINETEEN

As we walked, Mr. James filled in details he'd learned from his phone conversation.

"Mercy tried to contact us, but she didn't know where we were or how to find us," Mr. James said. "Then she saw you on TV."

The moment I met Stella, I felt a strong connection with her. I was sure she felt the same thing.

A memory came back to me then. "Oh, Mr. James, the day she got adopted, she was so happy. But also sad. Just before she left the shelter, she looked back at me. A big tear rolled down her cheek. Do you think, somehow, she knew?"

"I think we never completely forget the ones we've loved and lost. They're always a part of us. But don't dwell on the sad memories, okay?

You're going to see her again. Mercy and Stella are going to meet us at the finale."

I was so excited. My tail whacked Mr. James's chest so hard he hollered. "Mr. James, do you know what else this means?" I yelled, too excited to speak quietly. "My mom wasn't a bad dog. It wasn't her fault I ended up in a shelter. And I wasn't a bad pup. It wasn't my fault either."

"You're right, Ruby. We don't always know the reason why these things happen, but we shouldn't assume the worst." He looked off into the distance. "Maybe it wasn't necessarily my mother's fault I ended up in foster care, either."

"We won't assume the worst," I said, serious. "We don't know the whole story."

"My foot hurts." He sat down on a guardrail to rest. I suddenly noticed the way his lips were drawn and thinned out, as if he was trying to breathe through the pain. His face was pale too.

He checked his phone. "We've got fifty-eight miles to go."

My heart sank. I hadn't noticed how much pain he was in. "You won't make it fifty-eight steps, Mr. James. Want me to carry you? I can try."

He shook his head. "I'm thirty-five times your weight."

"Don't blame me! You're the one who had two slices of pie."

"We'll have to argue on the way. Got to get to Phoenix,"

Mr. James said. He sucked in his breath when he put weight on his right foot. Bending down, he reached for me to put me inside his jacket. I jumped back, out of his reach. No way was I going to let him carry me now.

Mr. James limped a few minutes and then took a break. He did that off and on for the rest of the day. My heart hurt worse than his foot, I think. Why did bad things happen to good people? In addition, why did bad news have to spoil the good?

We stopped for the night, and I hoped his foot would feel better in the morning. However, the next day, his foot was so swollen he couldn't get his shoe on until he removed the laces. His foot looked like a big, red football.

He kept walking anyway.

Five miles from the finish line, on the corner of Shea Boulevard and 104th, Mr. James fell.

He couldn't take another step.

I could tell the pain was unbearable.

"We have to cancel the rest of the walk, Mr. James." My heart was breaking. I wanted to see my mom again, and I wanted Mr. James to live out his dream. But pain doesn't care what we want.

"Ruby, I promised. We're going to make it to the finale, and you're going to see Stella."

"Mr. James, do you trust me?"

"You know I do, Ruby."

"Then trust me on this. I'll be right back."

I ran as fast as my legs could carry me, dodging in and out of people's legs on the crowded sidewalk, looking at street signs and shop names, looking for a sign with a big H on it. H is for hospital. I couldn't find one, though, not anywhere.

I sat on the curb for a moment to catch my breath. A man walked past me, chatting on his cell phone about the country singer who was due to come into town that afternoon.

I chased after him, and when I caught up, I grabbed his pant leg and pulled. Looking down, he held the phone away from his ear and stared at me. "What's wrong, pup?"

"I need you to follow me!" I yelled.

Though he probably heard barking instead of words, he let me lead him to Mr. James. When he noticed Mr. James's pained expression, he helped him stand.

The guy introduced himself as the DJ for a local radio station. He had been preparing to interview Mr. James that day and was wondering why he was late.

We loaded Mr. James into a car and rushed Mr. James to a podiatrist. That's a fancy name for a foot doctor.

The first thing Dr. Brian Allen did was ask Mr. James to

stand on a machine. Dr. Allen pressed a button, and a loud noise buzzed. He left the room for a few minutes. When he came back, he held an x-ray up to a light.

Mr. James winked at me. "Now I have an x-ray photo just like you, Ruby," he whispered.

"You've broken your foot," Dr. Allen said. Then he put a boot-cast on Mr. James.

Mr. James reached for his wallet, but the doctor waved it away. "No charge," Dr. Allen said. "It's my donation to your cause."

A few minutes later, the DJ drove Mr. James and me to the spot where Mr. James had collapsed.

"It's tempting to cheat and be driven to the finish line," Mr. James said. "But those kids are worth every step."

The faint sound of brass horns and snare drums danced in the distance. Several blocks away, apparently, a high school marching band was getting everyone riled up for the finale. The sounds of the band grew louder as we got closer.

Mr. James and I turned a corner past the Indian Steel Park and saw a mass of people lining both sides of the street, others leaning out of second-story windows. They cheered and clapped when they caught sight of us.

Mr. James tucked me inside his jacket. I protested—he didn't need any extra weight. But the crowd was so big and so excited there was a good chance someone would step on me.

A radio station mascot ran to meet us, wearing bowling shoes, a cowboy hat, and a barrel over his body held by shoulder straps. "Fifty more feet!" he chanted into a megaphone. The crowd repeated his words as Mr. James hobbled down the street on the boot cast.

"Forty more feet!"

A purple ribbon waved at us from the finish line.

"Thirty more feet!"

The crowd cheered and screamed. Just a few steps short of our goal, Mr. James, grinning from ear to ear, motioned for silence. The crowd quieted down.

"I walked all the way from Nashville, Tennessee, to right here. It took me seven months." He looked at me and winked. "And this little girl? She walked over half of it with me. I want all of you to know I couldn't have done this without her, and without all of you. We talk about people rescuing dogs, but sometimes we're the ones who need rescuing."

The crowd went wild, cheering.

He motioned for silence once more. "God made us in his image, and I believe He made dogs in his image too. Dogs have hearts of love, and God is love. Maybe that's why *dog* is *God* spelled backward! That's certainly why a dog is the only animal on the planet called man's best friend."

Everyone oohed and aahed and then cheered again. One lady in the front row dabbed at her eyes with a napkin.

"Are you ready to do this, Ruby?" Mr. James asked.

"I sure am!" I yelled back.

Somewhere in the crowd, I heard a familiar bark.

Could it be?

I heard the bark again and again and again. Through the crowd, I could see Stella! Her tail was wagging a hundred miles per hour.

"I see you!" I cried.

"I see you too, Ruby!" Stella called back. Now *my* tail was wagging a hundred miles per hour.

Mr. James took a step forward, toward the purple ribbon. Two foster children held the ends of the purple ribbon.

The crowd got silent again. Everyone had a camera or cell phone in the air, waiting for the moment when Mr. James would rip the ribbon. Mr. James took another step, then another step.

When he reached the ribbon, he grabbed it with both hands and ripped it in half, letting the ends flutter to the ground. The crowd roared with excitement.

The walk was finally over. Mr. James had walked 1,700 miles. I'd walked half of that with him. Or maybe half of half of half of that. But then, my legs are half of half of half the length of Mr. James's legs, so I figure I walked the same distance.

Right?

Mr. James picked me up and hugged me. I was so proud of him.

Through the crowd, I could see Stella. She was inching her way toward me. Once the photographers took all the photos they needed to take and the fans dissipated, I finally got a chance to reunite with her.

We hugged and cried. The tears continued to fall long after the final few pieces of confetti fell to the ground.

"I can't believe you

found me!" I cried. "We're eight hundred and fifty miles from the shelter!"

"Anything is possible if you refuse to give up hope. But I almost did. When the folks from the shelter said you were out walking, I didn't even know what that meant!"

"But you didn't give up?" I asked.

She shook her head. "You have to leave room for miracles, Ruby. One afternoon, I was lying on the floor in the den, thinking about my pups, when I heard your voice on the TV. 'That's her!' I shouted. 'That's him!' Ms. Mercy shouted.

"I looked at Willie, the long-haired dachshund that lived with Ms. Mercy, and said, 'That dog on the TV is my friend from the shelter that I told you about.'

"Ms. Mercy said to me, 'That man is the person who adopted your friend from the shelter.' That's when she told me you were my pup."

I licked her face, my tail wagging softly. "We're family."

Stella's eyes teared up. "Both of us being here together is a miracle. Just like with the foster care system and adoptions, it wasn't easy. Some people give up because the process is too hard."

She sounded sad, so I licked her cheek, and she wagged her tail.

Now it was Stella's turn to lick my face. "You had some big stumbling blocks too, but you turned them into stepping-stones. You should be proud of yourself."

"Oh, Stella, there hasn't been a day that's gone by that I haven't thought about you and wondered if you were okay. When I learned you were my mother, my heart broke even more for you. I knew there was something extra special about you when we first met in the shelter. I know it wasn't your fault I was placed there. I'm glad we're back together. *And God will restore the time the locusts have eaten.* That's a promise from the Bible."

Stella wagged her tail extra hard at that thought. "Enough tears! It's time to celebrate and dance in the sunshine!"

"Yep!" I wagged my tail just as hard. "Mr. James says we can use our gifts of experience to shine a light for others and help them find the way. And if those people shine their lights, imagine the impact that could have in this world."

"That's right, Ruby." Mr. James picked me up and twirled me around. "This isn't the finish line. This walk was only the first step. The sky is the limit."

"Wait a minute, Mr. James. Remember the poster at the Pie-O-Neer Café? There are footprints on the moon … right beside the American flag. So the sky is *not* the limit!"

I wagged my tail. I had never been so happy. I wagged my tail so much my wagger was going to be sore.

CHAPTER TWENTY

Southwest Airlines flew Mr. James and me home to Nashville.

I was hogging the window seat, but when a nice flight attendant carrying a tray of drinks stopped beside Mr. James, she got my attention. She wore a pin on her uniform in the shape of a heart with wings.

"Would you like something to drink?" she asked.

"Sure. I would like a Coca-Cola," Mr. James answered. "Ruby would like some fresh water with no ice, please."

She handed our beverages to us, each with a napkin that had a heart on it, then headed down the aisle to take care of other passengers.

"Mr. James," I said, "look! Southwest Airlines has a heart on their napkins."

"It's part of their logo," he said.

"I have two hearts on my chest. And we were both born in Texas."

"Well, Ruby, Southwest Airlines is the most lovable airline and you are the most lovable dog on the planet." He grinned at me and then continued, lowering his voice. "Southwest has such a big heart for foster care, they donated this flight to us."

"Maybe that's why I have two hearts, Mr. James."

He raised his eyebrows.

"I'm supposed to do what Southwest Airlines does— share the love!"

I couldn't believe my eyes. Mr. James's house looked like a tree. I mean, *our* house looked like a tree.

I was still getting used to being adopted, I guess.

"Why does your house sit on top of another house?" I asked.

"It's a two-story cabin."

As soon as we walked inside, I sniffed every inch of the bottom house, and each step going up the stairs, and every inch of the second house. There were no dog smells anywhere. Clearly Mr. James had never had a dog before.

When I came downstairs, Mr. James was brewing coffee and going through a giant stack of mail. I ran outside.

The backyard was just as big as I had imagined, and a weeping willow tree cast long shadows in the afternoon sun. I ran around as hard and fast as I could, just like that day in the rest area.

Mr. James came out and saw me. He laughed and clapped and even ran with me. He couldn't keep up, though, because I'm just that fast—and he still had a broken foot.

Finally, I flopped over onto my side, panting hard and getting a little emotional.

"Ruby, why are you crying?"

"Mr. James, I'm just so happy and so thankful for this home and this big yard. You could have chosen any dog in the world, but you chose me. These are happy tears!"

We walked back into the house, and Mr. James set a bowl down on the floor. It was one of many gifts we'd received from the nice foster kids at the airport holding posters. On the side of the bowl was written "Royalty equals loyalty."

When I cocked my head, Mr. James explained, "Ruby, that means when you're good to others they'll be good to you."

After a sip of cool water, I headed into the living room to find a comfy spot to lie down. I tested the couch, then a chair, then the carpet, then jumped back onto the couch.

"Ruby!" Mr. James yelled.

I jumped off the couch, worried he was mad.

But he had a big grin on his face. "Gina just called and asked if I'll perform at the Ryman Auditorium tonight."

"Who's Gina?"

"She books the talent for all the *Opry* shows. She's a single mom also who adopted a beautiful little girl named Eden from Ethiopia."

"She adopted Eden all by herself?"

"Yep, she sure did. Their story is just like ours, Ruby. It only takes one person to make a difference in someone else's life. She heard I just got back from the walk and wants me to sing on the Ryman Auditorium stage tonight."

"We just got home! Now we're leaving again?"

"Welcome to my world, Ruby."

I looked longingly at the couch, then followed Mr. James out the door.

We walked up an alley to the back entrance of the Ryman Auditorium. A police officer stood in the archway under the word "Ryman," guarding the back door.

Maybe the red carpet was inside.

"Good to see you, Mr. James." The policeman shook hands with Mr. James and let us pass.

We walked through the back door and up the steps of

the Ryman Auditorium, where another police officer was waiting for us.

"You're in room number three, Mr. James," he said, pointing down the hall.

While the officer filled out some paperwork and handed me a guest badge, I could hear a man down the hall talking. He sounded just like one of those guys on the radio. "The *Grand Ole Opry* is brought to you by Dollar General," he said.

Mr. James's face lit up. "Ruby, that's Eddie Stubbs at the podium. He sure is a great radio host, isn't he? Mr. Stubbs, Bill Cody, and Mike Terry are the best in the business."

The audience cheered when a song began, then a few minutes later, they cheered again.

"And that was 'Riders in the Sky,'" the announcer, Mr. Stubbs, said. "Up next, we have a young man who has just completed a walk halfway across America to raise awareness for foster children aging out of foster care."

I stamped all four paws. "That's you, Mr. James. He's talking about you."

"He and his little dog, Ruby, are here tonight, so please welcome them."

The crowd cheered.

"And that's you too, Ruby," Mr. James said.

My eyes went wide, and the room began to swim around me. Mr. James had not told me I would have to go onstage.

"Do you hear that noise?" I whispered. "My heart is pounding out of my chest, Mr. James."

"That's okay. You have two hearts, remember? Just wave at the crowd and stand beside me in the circle. Let's go."

We stepped on stage into the spotlight. At our feet was a circle, and Mr. James walked into it. "Every legend in the business has stood here," he whispered.

The crowd continued to cheer. The noise was so loud Mr. Stubbs couldn't say anything for a minute, so Mr. James pointed to the band. "That's Jimmy Capps back there on the guitar, Ruby. He's a legend."

I nodded. Mr. Capps waved hello, and I mouthed the word *help*. He just winked at me. He seemed to think I was an old pro.

Mr. James spoke to the crowd. "Hello, everyone. It's an honor being here tonight. I'm going to play a song I wrote during my walk. It's called 'Ruby.'"

Eddie Bayers yelled out, "One, two, three," as he knocked his drumsticks together. The Opry house band started playing.

I watched the happy faces in the crowd and then turned to watch the band playing. They looked happy too. The spotlight was warm and bright, and suddenly I wasn't frightened anymore.

These people really loved Mr. James. Of course, if they only knew what his socks smelled like, they wouldn't be acting this crazy. Cameras clicked, and Mr. James sang on as I wagged my tail.

After the song ended, Mr. James thanked the band, then turned to face the crowd. "Thank you very much for having me and my little dog, Ruby." He bowed to the audience, and they roared again.

We quickly exited the stage and Mr. Stubbs went on with the show.

"The next portion of the *Grand Ole Opry* is brought to you by Humana. Ladies and gentlemen, welcome Ricky Skaggs." His voice disappeared behind us as we walked toward the dressing room.

"It's hard to believe no one rehearses with the Opry house band before performing with them on stage. You just hand them a piece of sheet music and they read the notes. That's how good those musicians and background singers are," Mr. James said.

I could tell he was still excited. So was I, but not about the musicians. "Mr. James, did you write that song about me?"

"I sure did, Ruby. I wrote it during our walk. I didn't say anything about it earlier because I wanted it to be a surprise."

"Well, that was the most amazing, stupendous, spectacular surprise ever." I ran around in circles, wagging my tail. Then I sprinted down the hallway and back three times.

"Ruby, stop," Mr. James whispered, stifling a laugh. "They don't allow loud talking, running, or horseplay backstage. We'll get in big trouble! After we get outside we can celebrate as loud as we want to."

As soon as the back door opened into the alley, I yelled, "Yahoo!"

Mr. James was right behind me and yelled, "Yeeeee-haw!"

Everyone across the alley at Jack's Barbecue whipped their heads around and stared at us. I froze, then slowly turned my head around and looked at Mr. James. I was so embarrassed.

"What's wrong, Ruby?" Mr. James asked as we walked past the spectators.

"Yee-haw? Really, Mr. James?" I said.

We both busted out laughing and laughed all the way back to the truck.

We drove away from the Ryman Auditorium through the neon lights and tourists crowding Broadway. The Nashville skyline finally disappeared in the rearview mirror as we drove on I-65 South toward home.

"I'm so proud of you, Mr. James."

"I'm proud of you also, Ruby. It's been an amazing few months, hasn't it?"

I nodded.

"I can't wait to get home. It's been seven months since I've slept in my own bed," Mr. James said. "And you have a comfortable little bed on the floor beside my bed. That's where you'll sleep tonight."

"Well, we'll see about that." I thought about the couch. Maybe I would save that spot for afternoon naps. Mr. James had two pillows on his bed. He couldn't use both of them, could he?

🐾

The ceiling fan reminded me of that tornado spinning around and around outside of White Deer, Texas. But I was thankful to finally have a nice, comfortable home. The shelter was just a bad memory now. The only thing that could make life any better would be if Mr. James bought some more of those Goldfish crackers and fed them to me. Goldfish crackers were my favorite. I cocked one ear.

Downstairs, Mr. James was strumming an acoustic guitar. I'd have to get up off my puffy white pillow and drag myself downstairs before he ate all the Goldfish crackers. They were his favorite too.

Sighing, I stood up and walked to the foot of the bed, then hopped down onto the top of a footlocker Mr. James had made when he was in high school. Once on the hardwood floor, I stretched my back and legs, yawned, and headed down the hardwood stairs.

Mr. James was sitting on the couch, strumming a black guitar. Next to him was his phone.

"Recording another song?" I asked.

"Yeah," he said, then crammed a handful of Goldfish crackers into his mouth.

I jumped up onto the couch.

Mr. James got a serious look in his eyes. "Ruby, I need to talk to you about something very important."

I gulped. Had I been eating too many Goldfish crackers? Did I need to cut back? I could still fit into that ridiculous sweater he bought me last month. Maybe I was eating too many purple popsicles.

"Ruby …"

There was a long pause. I'd never felt so nervous.

"How do you feel about adopting another dog?"

Mr. James gave a very long explanation that felt like an

apology. I didn't really hear much of what he said because I was too excited.

"Ruby, you're perfect. Adopting another dog has nothing to do with you. It's just—"

"I love the idea," I interrupted.

"You do? I mean, I wasn't really sure how you were going to take it."

"Mr. James. Just because you helped me doesn't mean you should stop there. We should help others as much as we possibly can. Share the love, right?"

"James 1:27 says we're supposed to help the orphans. I think that means orphan doggies too."

I stared at him. "Wait. Did you say James 1:27? Your name is James, and my number in the shelter was 127."

Mr. James's eyes got big. "Ruby, that must be a sign! Let's go to the shelter right now." He set his guitar down on the couch.

I took a deep breath. I didn't want to go back to the shelter. Not for as long as I lived.

Mr. James held out his arms to me.

I did belong in his arms, I realized, and as long as he was with me, I didn't have to be afraid anymore.

CHAPTER TWENTY-ONE

Mr. James set me on the seat beside him in the truck. He turned the key, and as the engine rumbled to life, he cranked his head to the side. Then he threw his arm over the burlap-covered bench seat and backed the truck out of the driveway.

"I need to widen this driveway," he mumbled.

"Mr. James, why do we park on a driveway and drive on a parkway?"

"The same reason feet smell and noses run."

"Gross! That does not make any sense whatsoever." I looked out the window. "Are we there yet?"

"We're still in the driveway, Ruby."

"Oh. Sorry."

He backed the truck onto a long dirt road and then turned for the main road. He looked at me and grinned. "You're right, you know. Many things don't make sense, Ruby. For example, there are 2.2 billion self-proclaimed Christians and 153 million orphans in the world. If God's desire is for us to care for the orphans, then why are there still so many who need help?"

"Wow! Just imagine if even half of the population helped. There wouldn't be any orphans," I said.

"Or even if half of half of half of us helped," he replied.

I glanced out the window, then back at Mr. James. "Are we there yet?"

"Just enjoy the ride, Ruby."

We were flying down the highway now. Mr. James rolled down the window on my side so I could stick my head out and let the wind blow in my face. Just like I had dreamed about back at the shelter. When I had no idea what my dream would look like in real life.

My dreams had come true. I had a family, a home, and a truck window to stick my head out when we were driving. I glanced over at Mr. James. If I squinted hard enough, I could still see the tan lines from the ski goggles he wore on our first day together.

He was crazy, all right. He was my kind of crazy.

"Are we getting close to the shelter?" I asked.

"For the third time, we're almost there."

When we arrived, I jumped out of the truck and ran to the front door of the shelter, where a cute little dog was lying in a cage on a piece of cardboard. He looked nervous. I knew how he felt. And I knew exactly what he was thinking.

I stopped in front of his cage, barking.

A shelter employee pulled him out of the cage and handed him to Mr. James. Mr. James set him down beside me. He was the cutest thing I had ever seen. Solid white with three black dots, two sparkling eyes, and a little black nose.

He was shaking with fear.

"It's going to be okay," I whispered in his ear. "Where's your towel? Do you want to bring it?"

He wouldn't look me in the eyes as he whispered, "I didn't get a towel. A bigger dog took the last one."

I licked his cheek. "That's all right. You can share mine."

His tail wagged, but just barely.

"What's your name?" I asked.

He looked down at the tag hanging from his collar. "2222," he replied.

"That's a number, silly. You're not a number, not anymore," I said. "You're family now."

On the way back home, Mr. James received a phone call from Stella's mom.

"I think Ms. Mercy is going to bring Stella to visit," Mr. James said after he hung up.

"Stella's mom is single, isn't she?" I wiggled my eyebrows. The new guy looked back and forth between me and Mr. James. I would have to fill him in later.

"Yes. She's also beautiful. And most important, she's a Christian."

Mr. James rolled down the window, and I stuck my nose out as far as I could reach. My ears flapped just like Parker the Barker's did.

My new little

friend crawled up beside me. "Where are we going?" he whispered.

"Home," I said, and for the first time I understood how beautiful that word really was. I glanced over at Mr. James, then looked back at my new friend. "We're going home."

He wiggled closer to me and pushed his nose out the window. He wasn't shaking now.

Somewhere in the distance, I heard a train and its horn, and my thoughts flew to all those orphans, both pups and people, who were still out there waiting for their forever homes. The sun began its long descent over the horizon, but I wasn't afraid of the lonely nights anymore. Turns out, when love finally finds you, that's not the end.

Happily ever after? That's just the beginning.

Share Ruby's heart!

✂ cut here

Ruby wants you to share the important message of this book with others. Please cut out this page and give it to a friend.

Hi friend!

I loved this book and think you'll love it too. Learn more by visiting RubyTheFosterDog.com

You can also check out what's happening with Ruby at
Twitter: @RubyFosterDog
Instagram.com/RubyTheFosterDog

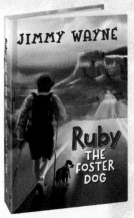

JIMMY WAYNE is a former foster kid turned award-winning country music artist whose songs and story highlight his mission to raise awareness for children in foster care. Jimmy's hits include "Stay Gone," "Paper Angels," "I Love You This Much," and "Do You Believe Me Now," which earned BMI's prestigious Million-Air Award for receiving one million radio spins in America. In 2009 Jimmy toured with Brad Paisley and recorded "Sara Smile" with rock 'n roll Hall of Fame duo Daryl Hall and John Oates.

In 2010 Jimmy walked halfway across America (from Nashville to Phoenix) to raise awareness for kids aging out of the foster-care system. In 2012 Jimmy helped get legislative bills passed extending the age of foster care to twenty-one in California, Tennessee, North Carolina, Ohio. In 2014 he released *Walk to Beautiful: The Power of Love and a Homeless Kid Who Found The Way*, a three-time *New York Times* bestselling memoir, which recently crossed the 100,000 print sales milestone. In 2016 he received the prestigious Points of Light award from President George W. Bush (41), and in 2017 he received an honorary Doctorate of Humane Letters from William Woods University.

Jimmy has performed on the Grand Ole Opry more than 215 times. He lives in Nashville and continues to work tirelessly on behalf of at-risk foster youth by performing, writing books, and keynote speaking. Jimmy's ultimate goal is to build transitional homes for youth who age out of foster care without a place to go.

To connect with Jimmy and learn more about his awareness campaign, Project Meet Me Halfway, please visit:

JimmyWayne.com
Facebook.com/JimmyWayneOfficial
Twitter.com/JimmyWayne
Instagram/JimmyWayneOfficial
ProjectMMH.org